Spontaneity

GW00566836

Psychoanalytic theory frequently explains psychopathology from the perspectives of either inadequate early care or as the result of environmental factors. In this book the author suggests that poor mental health can be a result of our incapacity to respond to internal and external stimuli, and she indicates that spontaneity is essential in the development of many aspects of the self.

Gemma Corradi Fiumara draws on a wealth of clinical and theoretical experience to demonstrate that it is not what happens to us, but how we react to these events, that forms who we are. *Spontaneity* presents an original approach to issues of agency, spontaneity and creativity in psychoanalysis by exploring areas including:

- active internalization
- paradox
- forgiveness
- responsibility
- empathy
- self-decreation.

This book will be essential reading for psychoanalysts, psychotherapists, philosophers and psychologists. It will also prove to be engaging for those interested in psychoanalytic theory and theories of subjectivity.

Gemma Corradi Fiumara is a former professor of philosophy at the Third University of Rome and a training analyst with the Italian Psychoanalytic Society. Her previous books include *The Symbolic Function, The Other Side of Language, The Metaphoric Process* and *The Mind's Affective Life*.

Spontaneity

A Psychoanalytic Inquiry

Gemma Corradi Fiumara

Routledge
Taylor & Francis Group

LONDON AND NEW YORK

First published 2009 by Routledge
27 Church Road, Hove, East Sussex BN3 2FA

Simultaneously published in the USA and Canada
by Routledge
270 Madison Avenue, New York, NY 10016

Routledge is an imprint of the Taylor & Francis Group, an Informa business

© 2009 Gemma Corradi Fiumara

Typeset in Times by Garfield Morgan, Swansea, West Glamorgan
Printed and bound in Great Britain by T J International Ltd, Padstow,
Cornwall
Paperback cover design by Gerald Myers

This publication has been produced with paper manufactured to strict
environmental standards and with pulp derived from sustainable forests.

British Library Cataloguing in Publication Data
A catalogue record for this book is available from the British Library

Library of Congress Cataloging-in-Publication Data
Corradi Fiumara, Gemma.
    Spontaneity : a psychoanalytic enquiry / Gemma Corradi Fiumara. – 1st ed.
        p. cm.
    Includes bibliographical references and index.
    ISBN 978-0-415-49268-3 (hardback) – ISBN 978-0-415-49269-0 (pbk.) 1.
Individuation (Psychology) 2. Psychoanalysis and philosophy. 3. Human
information processing. 4. Subjectivity. I. Title.
    BF175.5.I53C67 2009
    155.2'105–dc22

                                                              2008049254

ISBN: 978-0-415-49268-3 (hbk)
ISBN: 978-0-415-49269-0 (pbk)

For my brave daughter Linda

Contents

Chapter 1

Introductory remarks

Preliminary remarks

In the continuing stream of psychoanalytic developments, we can observe its tendency to flow in a series of conversations privileging first one conception and then another, with each series, perhaps, constituting a structure of binary oppositions. Psychoanalysis has in fact initiated creating the space for unconscious psychic life in a cultural background of conscious rationality. In the subsequent perspective of libidinal instincts, the perplexing role of destructive drives also came to be included. And then, in an outlook of defence against the irruption of drives into the ego, a space was allowed for the need of, and defence from, other persons – the celebrated *objects* of the psychoanalytic vocabulary. After that, the universe of transference has had to somehow include countertransference. And perhaps now a psychoanalytic culture of determinism and causal relations may finally come to interact with the essential question of spontaneity.

Reflections on the inner dynamics of psychic life are often intended as personal companions in the evaluation of the complexive quality of clinical work. And when one 'happens' to introduce a specific word – say, 'spontaneity' – in the process of taking notes from thoughts, then the written term proceeds to resonate and to function as a conceptual magnet in the re-evaluation of experience. For, in fact, we cannot ask the question 'What is spontaneity?' It only exists as a worthy concern if we are interested in the quest and question of spontaneous actions. And although it cannot be approached as a topic of empirical research, once our attention, or insight, has captured its psychic intensity it will ultimately enhance the quality of clinical observation.

Rigidly adhering to any cultural construct, we come to separate 'good' theory from 'bad' theory according to concrete agglomerations of contents, rather than according to inner currents that run through the laborious activities of both individuals and institutions. Elaborating differences requires more work than making partitions according to agglomerative entities. If psychoanalysis is not a humble self-questioning venture that allows itself to be constantly challenged by the enigmatic aspects of mental life – as, for instance, spontaneity – then it may well metamorphose into a most hubristic form of thought. Without engaging the unconscious, in fact, our self-interrogation may never be vigilant enough. Only by positing unconscious psychic life as that which resists consciousness and rational thought will we be humble enough to pursue the question of our motives, fears and potentials.[1] But then, while a specific problem can be thought of as something that we can face and confront, the basic questions of psycho-analytic research – subjective agency, for instance – are such that they include the questioner in the question, in the sense that the immense complexity of the inquirer cannot be excluded.

And thus psychoanalysis turns out to be both an addressive and an observational discipline: knowers are not spectators of distinct and distant 'objects of knowledge' but engaged participants in conversation with one another *and* with what they seek to know. Every thought, theory or hypothesis is an answer to a very human question – not an abstract or 'perennial' question, but one that is posed out of specific psychological vicissitudes.[2] One way to appreciate the contribution of psychoanalysis to the quest(ion) of spontaneity is to see it as indicating that we have somehow reiteratively tried to pursue an essential aspiration to spontaneity. Though it may not often seem so, each of us is already in the midst of a life of passionate, personal quests. Although these pursuits may only be expressed in a rudimentary way, they nonetheless inspire our inner lives: if you want to do something badly enough, you just do it and worry later.

We do not cease to ask questions, and we often try to pose them while striving to arrive at the virtual place in which we believe the source of answers can be found. Questioning also emancipates us from the attraction of 'absolute' knowledge, the sort of 'permanent' knowledge that does not usually oppress psychoanalysis but does not spare it either.[3] Along with the acquisition of knowledge there is at work a parallel effort to make it explicit through one's own voice; this book is therefore perhaps no more than an attempt to elaborate old issues in such a way that they can be visited, re-visited and visited again.

Current literature is often so focused on the external causes of self-formation, pathology and health that we may be tempted to eclipse the role of inner factors. Outer and inner determinants are, of course, both at work, but inner sources of early mental growth are more often vulnerable to obscurity. This book is an attempt to create a more balanced approach. If we attribute the narcissistic root of pathology to inadequate early care, we almost become ensnared in a paranoid theory of psychic life whereby all negativity derives from sources placed somewhere 'out there'. But then, if we attribute basic pathology to the way in which events are internalized by developing subjects, to the response of the person involved, then there is the risk of lapsing into a moralistic, judgemental way of theorizing. As is known, the psychoanalytic literature abounds in clinical and theoretical ventures attempting to investigate causal precedents that determine any shadow of illness. This is the ultimate logic: in the early relational vicissitudes lies the genesis of pathological narcissism in the sense that it is the quality of caretaking that basically determines and shapes mental development. This outlook seems to prevent the awareness of any degree of early subjective agency. The assumption sustaining this outlook is that the influence of primal care in fact ultimately determines the psychic destiny of all creatures. We try to integrate this unduly deterministic scenario through an exploration of spontaneity, agency, intentionality – that 'easily bruised creativity'[4] – which we do not regard as an exclusively adult function. But if the inchoate self is shattered by trauma against its will, how could we say that narcissistic inclinations can be eschewed? As usual, it is a question of proportions, choices and vicissitudes. But then, if narcissism is 'chosen', it should be possible for that choice to be reversed, and life may grant opportunities to reverse that problematic anti-object option.[5] This view is at variance with a deterministic outlook whereby a pathological narcissistic structure is entirely caused by cumulative traumatic circumstances. In this view it is even more difficult to see how the narcissistic 'choice' can be reversed, for in fact there is apparently no previous choice that can subsequently be recanted.

In an attempt to appreciate a pre-theoretical spontaneous concern for our psychic well-being we could perhaps consider that a number of human beings have been labouring with the 'essentials of psychoanalysis' from time immemorial. One of the shortcomings of our definitory tendencies is that we regard disciplinary domains – such as psychoanalysis – as absorbing all of our personal, spontaneous commitment to the health of our inner life. If, for instance, we think of intellectual history in terms of what the official 'philosophers' have been doing, then the majority of creatures appear as excluded from it – and culturally silenced. But if we conceive of our intellectual heritage as a story of struggle for psychic survival, truth and values, then we could have doubts about clearly defined roles and boundaries in human efforts. If we do not separate the daily travail of dealing with inner suffering and aspirations from the elitist rendition of these efforts, we are in a better position to ask about what the vast majority of people may have been doing; this is an alternative to simply investigating what any intellectual elite was saying that they were doing or ought to be doing.

That we meet a degree of expressive rigidity and reluctance in ourselves, in patients and in society is too obvious to require proof. And thus the question is whether or not we can actually talk about the genesis of our psychic problems. We may be at ease discussing crucial issues with colleagues who come from similar (pathological) backgrounds or share similar convictions. But in the interests of maintaining civility we may avoid touching on controversial issues with persons of markedly dissimilar persuasions. We may even use the psychoanalytic jargon precisely in order not to talk. Unfortunately such silence and distancing maintains only a veneer of cultural plausibility; what are actually maintained are ignorance and misunderstanding.

The quest(ion) of spontaneity

By saying 'the quest(ion)' of spontaneity – that is, by welding together quests and questions – we try to speak of two interlocking approaches. We make no effort to comprehend that which we neither value nor look for; but if we are tentatively in quest of spontaneity, then we shall strive to understand – and pose the question.

And thus spontaneity is neither reified, of course, nor simply regarded as a liminal, evanescent and insubstantial mental feature. Its elusiveness should not be regarded as a failure of method or theory. It is a sign instead of what spontaneity is: an essential and perhaps most important quality of psychic life, sustaining all forms of creativity. In fact, as soon as spontaneity is romanticized, we lose it. The development of spontaneity, paradoxically, leaves scars.

The quest for spontaneity is the process of allowing the uniquely personal features – the cipher, the 'I' – to emerge in the personality;[6] and this is a challenge that confronts all of us and may always have been present. This quest is now becoming a priority, as spontaneity is silently and ubiquitously under attack by the homogenizing effect of mass culture and by the contagion of indifference in all areas. Not only is the issue clinically essential, it is becoming culturally urgent.[7]

We might easily agree with this diagnosis of our times, and anyone could say that it is true, that he was about to say so himself and that he had already thought about it. And so the point is how we can be affected by this awareness. A reader may ask why is someone writing the book that she is reading, and, if she can appreciate the book, she may wonder why she should not be the person who has written it. And thus by resorting to our spontaneous epistemophily we can gain a better grasp of the ever-decreasing difference between the roles of reader and writer. Both appear to be ultimately involved in the question.

The theoretical contents of psychoanalytic discourses are not what we could call natural entities; such theoretical objects need to be constructed and developed. Once we are able to capture these fresh focuses of attention, then 'something' becomes more visible and audible in clinical research. Throughout this book runs the theme that spontaneous subjective agency is often one of these elusive aspects of our mind's life. We can tentatively 'read' this issue in disparate analytic contributions but in a form that does not allow a clear view of the problem. The attempt here is to render the question of subjective agency more clinically conspicuous. Although it seems like a very roundabout route, one could say that we have to 're-invent' psychoanalysis through our wayward wanderings before we can come back to clinical questions with a more spontaneous and direct per-spective. When we come back we may realize that the questions we have been asking about the mind have been far too narrowly conceived. This laborious approach contributes to an expanded 'objectivity' and to the encounter with ever-new dimensions of psychic life.

Fromm would say that we approach here 'one of the most difficult problems of psychology: the problem of spontaneity.'[8] He reminds us that spontaneous activity is 'free' activity of the self and that it implies, psychologically, what the Latin expression *sua sponte* literally means: of one's own free will, of one's own accord. We never seem quite able to fathom these depths fully. Sooner or later we inevitably run into an enig-matic core. The fullness of spontaneity is far from naturally comprehen-sible. But then, it could be that we are looking at it in the wrong way: we say that if we can solve all of our problems then we could live spon-taneously, instead of saying that if we can live with our problems we could move in the direction of spontaneity.

It may seem ironic to speak of spontaneity when for the majority of humankind there is nothing that it can choose or produce and nothing that it can earn or acquire. And so we could consider the question of spontaneity as the 'blessing' of those who can reasonably survive and of those who are resourceful enough not to opt for one or the other of the illusive ends of the gradient between 'freedom' and 'determinism' – a 'blessing' for those who manage to move forward and backward on this virtual line. This 'most difficult of the problems of psychology' appeals profoundly to everyone who is not so benumbed that he has lost the ability to perceive it. In fact, there is nothing more attractive or convincing than spontaneity, something admired to the extreme of envy, in whomever it may be recognized. Also, we com-monly think of the mind as a creation of our living body, aimed at consent-ing survival. And yet in the admiration of spontaneity we seem to perceive that this mental attitude, conversely, almost shapes and informs our living bodies. There is thus a pervasive question asked here, namely why this potential is not developed, why spontaneity for the most part is evaded or attacked. Symington synthetically says: 'It is essential to reach the real good, the *spontaneous* action within a person, and to give that our full support. I am struck by how much we therapists are taken in by the fake good.'[9]

On determinism

Of course, we constantly do our best in the search of determinants of pathology. And yet when a course of inquiry is seriously pursued, there is also something that is not considered or is altogether ignored. This may seem obvious in general. But the question is whether what is not tackled might lead to the crucial element that we most need to include and investigate. Bernardi remarks that there is no point in hoping not to be subject to our paradigms. What matters is to be aware of how much they condition our ability to observe and think: while opening certain horizons, they also close off others. 'The area that is most clear in each paradigm is also its blind spot; what they help us to think about is also what they cannot stop thinking about.'[10] And so we should frequently return from the domain of theory to the world of daily life and try to see how we are actually placed within our own paradigms. Assessing this placement could be one of our major goals. What form this effort will take we cannot predict. However, it is sufficient and truly consoling to know that whatever form it takes, the psychic life it describes will always remain richer than its description.

Insistence on situatedness is in a sense more honest than the 'myth' of causality, where a coercive assumption persists to the effect that theory-neutral, value-free scientific knowledge is possible not just for medium-sized tangible objects but for mental life as well. According to von Wright, the determinist tendencies present in the great traditions of the past survive in the neo-positivistic aspirations of a unitary science, encompassing both natural and human domains – thus obscuring the multiple forms in which the human condition is expressed.[11] As is known, the Enlightenment notion of science was imperialistic from the outset – it was associated with the ambitious claims of infallibility and of the formal unity of the whole enterprise.

Some contemporary views, however, recognize that these soaring ambitions cannot be achieved and also that they actually do not need to be. Rationality, in fact, does not require us to be infallible, to have all of our knowledge tightly organized on the model of empirical science. And yet we are still occasionally vexed by the idea that these ambitious principles are necessary; they thus come to function almost as 'epistemic idols'.[12] The internalized version of these idols carries with it the ambitions that they exhibit and the causalistic premises that they require; it tells us basically that all of our mental life is to be causally explainable. We thus often reduce people's motives to yet other underlying motives that are perhaps 'cruder' and more specifically causal than those usually admitted. We try to move from motives to causes. And yet, this sort of search for underlying causes is not unjustified. It is often called for, but it can be practised indiscriminately and wildly. Just consider the 'delight' of showing others up as moral frauds combined with the intellectual satisfaction of extending the influence of one's guiding idols. And thus, although reduction is often a useful instrument, not all reductions are enlightening or sensible. An illuminating example of insightful reduction can be read in Freud's work on narcissism: 'Parental love, which is so moving and at bottom so childish, is nothing but the parents' narcissism born again.'[13]

Schaefer, for instance, could be seen as aiming to substitute the 'physico-chemical' deterministic model with 'action language' based on choices and intentions. Schaefer's contribution is not inclined to nouns such as 'identi-fication', 'internalization', 'introjection', for his focus is more on emotional actions.[14] Such powerful terms may ultimately conceal the psychic actions that we perform or fail to perform. But, of course, it is not a question of replacing a putative Freudian deterministic outlook with an approach of intentionality, choice and purpose. The suggestion is that we can function with both. Determinism alone cannot explain much; but then, since we are embodied creatures essentially inseparable from drives, the ideas of freedom and intentionality – per se – would be meaningless. Similarly, when the more profound aspects of the inner life are concerned, the stark realism of the positivistic tradition becomes riddled with evasion and self-deception. Perhaps all in the name of maintaining high standards of scientific rigour and cohesion and of avoiding contaminations, the members of a profession may strive to reassure themselves that their theories are adequate, con-sistent and effective – thus remaining innocently ignorant.[15]

But then, if behaviour and pathology were so heavily determined, it would not even make sense to speak of strategizing therapies, options, efforts or aspirations. We are often inclined to think that narcissists are subjects who have been traumatized at an early age and that this is suffi-cient to explain their condition. Perhaps we could more productively think that it is not the cumulative trauma alone, but the individual's response to it that constitutes the origin of narcissistic 'relations'.[16] The creature is somehow responding to life events, and it is this crucial factor that we tend to underestimate and perhaps ignore – to the detriment of clinical acumen. We could be therapeutically more effective if we could also think in this ulterior perspective. The idea of spontaneity and inner actions – rather than mere reactions – can be a guideline in the exploration of narcissistic afflictions.[17] Ignoring this essential element might hinder our understanding of the mind's life.

Our innumerable endeavours to probe the genesis of pathology can be epistemically overwhelming in the sense that we ceaselessly look for deter-minants and causal connections. The prevalence of this outlook, in fact, may obscure our potential for spontaneity, agency, intentionality and initiative. As long as the search for determinants does tacitly prevail, subjective agency remains vulnerable to obscurity to the point of transforming analytic knowledge into a massive apparatus for sanctioning passivity, hopelessness and resignation. Also, it may ultimately encourage rigid demands of com-pensation in an inner atmosphere of entitlement. Of course, there can be instances in which the inchoate self is so severely damaged by early neglect and abuse that there can hardly be any responsive attitude; generally speak-ing, though, we can perhaps achieve a more enlightening perspective of things if we posit the presence of some elemental, minimal agentive functions.

In a classical view we could say that subjective agency is the relative capacity of individuals to behave or believe in conformance with, in contradiction to, in addition to, or without regard for what is perceived to be environmental or biological determinants. But then, with the advent of psychoanalytic culture we attentively thematize unconscious mental life and early vicissitudes in such a way that we more easily recognize the omnipotent hubris of our western mind. But the whole enterprise can also be utilized for purposes of constructing paranoid-like scripts that attribute our limits and pathology entirely to external causes. And thus only reluctantly may we explore this obscured agentive feature of our subjectivity. The narcissistic organization, for instance, can be thought of as always being caused by others – while we are not able to recognize the life-enhancing contribution of the other as such. The narcissistic route may be taken on the basis of one's response to trauma. Of course, narcissistic disorders often emerge from a traumatic scenario, but it is probably the quality of response to it by the subject that 'decides' whether or not a narcissistic default or forfeiture of the self will occur. And still, the devastated patients forever condemning the inadequacy or viciousness of their primordial objects are actually persons who do not give up analysis and constantly struggle in its pursuit – wilful subjects indeed.

Apart from whatever genetic factors may be at work, pathological cases are appropriately regarded as the outcome of adverse and/or perverse primal interactions, and we constantly probe the enigmas of early infancy. But this is only a partial approach. Some inner constitutive personhood is generally assumed and even clearly observed. Pragmatically speaking, this conjoined outlook can serve us better in the exploration of our pathological vicissitudes.

Although we frequently refer to a stage in which self and not-self only gradually become distinguishable, the original condition of narcissism is focused upon by theorists and clinicians; we may, however, eclipse, or even obscure, the balance between the mutual influences of outer and inner reality. In this way the possible role of any originary agency and initiative is often ignored. This attitude is comparable to exploring Freud's twenty-three volumes in search of arguments revealing his alleged misogyny; at the same time, one may retrieve arguments clearly utilizable to make a case for authentic feminism. In Freud's proclaimed persuasion of 'scientific determinism', it is in fact possible to identify passages where he points to spontaneity, intentionality, agency, initiative and creative action. For the sake of example, we could just recall two pristine instances of this attitude. As early as 1889 Freud refers to 'personal free will' and 'freely aspiring mental activity' as concepts that can be utilized and entertained even by 'the most positive of determinists'.[18] And in 1901: 'According to our analyses it is not necessary to dispute the right to the feeling of conviction of having a free will.'[19]

Causes and reasons

As suggested by McDowell – a philosopher – we should outline some provisional distinction between phenomena that can be referred to the domain of 'causes' and those that can be grouped under the rule of 'reasons'.[20] If we resist a crudely naturalistic temptation to simply include the domain of reasons and motives into the logical space of causes, we can in fact attempt a differentiation; some psychic vicissitudes can best be explained in terms of causal laws, and still others can be tentatively understood in terms of motivational reasons. He also points out that spontaneity cannot possibly be thought of as participating in natural phenomena. In our sophisticated parlance, the 'more fundamental' realm of causes is often called 'hard', as opposed to the 'less fundamental' domain of reasons which is called 'soft'. This tactile metaphor seems to imply that the softer levels of psychic functioning are only provisional, in that they fall short of ultimate, 'hard' explanation, and that they are to be tolerated until the 'real' scientific account is available. And yet, if we could only think in terms of natural causes and were blind to reasons, it would ultimately be unreasonable to investigate the maturational evolution of our intelligence – in both an ontogenetic and a phylogenetic sense.

Von Wright – who too was a philosopher – points out that human action is both free and determined, that it is itself already a sign of its radical doubleness, of the fragility and dramatic nature intrinsic to the evolutionary human condition. The fashionable term 'compatibilism' names a relation that is anything but stable, anything but painless, perhaps the search for a balance that has always been sought and never achieved.[21] The dream of escaping from the dualism of freedom and determinism is not so much aimed at solving it, as it is to dissolve the illusion that it is possible to treat causes as if they were reasons, and to regard reasons as quasi-causes.

That there is need for caution is specifically illustrated by Rizzuto *et al.* in their argument that 'The aspects of motivation calling for clarification . . . include the basic definition of motivation, appetition, the relation of wish and motivation, the distinction of cause and motive, the relation of reasons and motives, the relation of motives to needs, the question of non-drive motivation, the expression of drive-like characteristics, and finally the status of motives as determining behaviour.'[22] This is no doubt an extensive task.

In discussing Kohut's view of internalization, Symington significantly remarks that he has no place for internal determinants: 'The predicate is that a person's psychopathology is due to unattuned selfobjects, so all the bad is out there and we have a theory with a paranoid base.'[23] The idea that some of our expectations and desires seem to imply teleological (as distinct from efficient) causes is abhorrent to several scholars of psychoanalysis. In particular, theorists and philosophers who have an interest in Freud may be disturbed by this 'unscientific intrusion', as they see it; but perhaps it should not be too summarily dismissed. In fact, analysts who are committed to explaining psychological phenomena through efficient causality alone might consider that such a framework is not entirely adequate to account for the inner vicissitudes that they are trying to share in their daily work.

Psychoanalytic outlooks seem to share a paradoxical perspective whereby the inchoate self is regarded as something at the mercy of external care-takers, while at the same time it should aspire to the subjectivity and agentiveness of parental figures. In Oliver's view, this perspective is not dissimilar from a colonizing attitude. In fact, any colonial propensity is based on the incongruence between denying the internal mind or soul of the colonized, on the one hand, and demanding that they internalize colonial values, on the other: 'The colonized status as human yet not human, as agent yet not agent, is part and parcel of its contradictory logic.'[24]

Chapter 2

Rethinking internalization

Internalization revisited

The process of internalization is briefly revisited here in order to emphasize its active, laborious quality. The features of intentionality, creativity and imagination – however minimal or inchoate – are frequently marginalized in the ongoing exploration of this topic. As 'internalization' includes aspects of processes such as identification and introjection, the term is used here to refer to the essential activity of assimilating and metabolizing experience for the sake of self-formation and psychic survival.

In Klein's view, as is known, the inchoate psyche appears ruled by two complementary dynamics: expulsion of inner contents in the sense of projection, and ingestion or absorption of outer living figures, in the sense of introjection. The pristine mind can be envisaged as preoccupied in the alternation of these two experiences. Whereas some theorists suggest that the developing individual simply turns away from outer frustrating figures, Klein insists that far from being ignored or repelled, these figures are intruded upon and attacked.[1] And then, to the extent that they are subsequently internalized, they precipitate in the form of persecutory inner objects. Whereas some analysts claim that frustrating outer figures are avoided as not being sufficiently good, or even bad, Klein emphasizes the way in which the infant may actually manage to *make* them bad.

Apart from the specific details of Klein's theory, what is relevant to the present context is the quasi-intentional, agentive function that is attributed to the developing individual. We could thus say that outer objects are transformed by our projections, and that internalized objects are consequently influenced by the quality of our previous attributions. There seems to be a recognition of the active propensities of the early ego, almost as if we were positing the existence of some pristine psychic agency; some theorists, however, appear to allow limited space for the intentional response of the infant. The present concern is in fact the agency, the activity, the personal involvement and the emotional actions sustaining internalization in the course of mental growth.

Freud had already sufficiently anticipated the subject's personal contribution in the process of internalization. In his revision of the early seduction theory, for instance, he came to recognize that the most relevant features of what his patients were confiding to him (and which he had regarded as essential to his theory) were not necessarily 'true'; what they introduced were more like relational responses. He realized that what mattered was not the factual event, but the personal experience that was actively internalized; he saw that even if an event had not actually taken place, what counted was indeed what his patients were *telling* him, or what was created by their minds.[2] He thought that he had known this all along, and he probably had, but then he could only overcome that difficulty by taking the idea more seriously than before. Parsons suggests that 'He either had to abandon his work or realize that what he had been doing was only a beginning. Accepting what his patients said, whether it was objectively true or not, really did matter in a way he had not seen until then.'[3]

In a narcissistic approach, the subject speaks of others as if they were 'natural facts' that can be mechanically reified; he does no more than assert that the 'other' is this or that way, without the slightest concern for his own psychic responsibility in the attribution of qualities. In Faimberg's view, the function of this attitude is to preserve the narcissistic cohesion and sometimes even the survival of the self.[4] Because of this narcissistic regulation, the subject eliminates the responsibility for his own relationship with the world; in this predicament the individual is bound to always designate others as the source of pain, and his own self as the source of pleasure and well-being. And Faimberg adds that the narcissistic approach is not sufficiently recognized as being linked to the specific attitudes of appropriation and intrusion. Also, when there is contradiction between an event described and the outer figures mechanically internalized, the contradictory event is quickly made to fit the mechanically reproduced figures, however much it may strain logical consistency.

Without the idea of some creativity in the process of internalization, we would be left with an abstract, pro forma exchange of positions. Without inner creativity only a reversal of the respective positions of power would be possible – and no psychic growth. When the outer figures are not 'sufficiently good', they may 'become' intrusive and obnoxious. In the position formed around this fear alone, the fragile self remains lodged in a paranoid stance towards the other, in which the adult's existence as an agent could only mean oppression of the infant. There are conditions imposed on the individual, as well as something that is creatively accomplished. Internalization probably participates in both activity and passivity. It is unfortunate, however, that the active aspects of internalization are often vulnerable to obscurity. Also, the use of the term 'fantasy' commonly carries the sense of something unreal, whereas action in fantasy is real psychological activity; it is activity that affects the emotional processes within the subject. When the early process of internalization amounts to an ingestion, implosion or incorporation, the resulting inner objects can only be felt as alien and debilitating parts of the self. By contrast, when the process is more creative than purely mechanical, then the inner objects have a life-enhancing capacity comparable to the affective quality infused in the act of internalization. From this outlook, some kernel of subjectivity is safeguarded as an escape from an encompassing mechanics of identification. If a minimal principle of subjective agency is allowed for, then we can be thought to aspire to the laborious development of psychic life; to some extent attacks can be transformed into mental suffering instead of being locked into the mechanics of automatic retaliation, expulsion and splitting.

Gaddini points out, in fact, that there is a 'lengthy and laborious' development of the capacity to generate internalizations and identifications; these are to be distinguished from the more primitive precursors of imitation, incorporation and ingestion.[5] An extreme account of internalization could be articulated in this way: individuals constitute themselves through the creative quality of their experiences. And thus identifications are not as mechanical as they are sometimes described; there seems to be some pristine filtering function at work whereby the individual almost appears to 'decide' whether or not something should be internalized – and in which way.

Symington reports that for many years he believed that narcissistic subjects had been traumatized at an early stage of development and that these experiences were sufficient for explaining their narcissistic rigidity; he now believes that the traumas of childhood are not sufficient per se to explain their narcissistic condition.[6] He thinks that its cause is not the trauma alone, but the individual's response to it. He believes that the individual has an emotional relation to the trauma: 'The basic structure of our minds lies in emotional action.'[7] He argues that the person is constantly responding to life events and that this is the crucial element that he had basically ignored to the detriment of his patients. From this ulterior perspective, he claims to be more effective in tackling narcissism.

Altieri also points out that it is often claimed that identifications depend on 'social grammars' and that these are woven into the relational work done in fostering the specific contents that we take on. But this is to ignore a great deal; this perspective must be somehow complemented by another stance that focuses on what is involved in our forging personal identities by making articulate how and why we develop certain ways of acting as makers of who we want to be.[8] It is at least arguable that we do not give an adequate account of self-formation if we dwell only on the play of different identifications: there is also a process of making the selections that establish personal identity. A sense of specific human agency working in the quest of identity is not frequently considered, and there is usually no mention of the possibility that judgement might enter into the process of making identifications.

When suffering people attempt the psychoanalytic venture, they gradually turn inward to their feelings, and it is a significant life step to do so. Contacting feelings as a result of absorbing interpretations is aimed at an inner itinerary of self re-creation; this requires a holistic sense of body–mind activity. It is from this potential that a series of actual inner shifts can arise. Perhaps we can best recognize this active, transformative response by observing patients who are naturally gifted and are proficient at it. Some analysands have the capacity to use interpretation in such a creative way that actual shifts of energy, recombinations and transformations of the inner organization can occur. There is therefore a need to explore this essential, beneficial propensity and to render it more conspicuous. To summarize it: it is not interpretation, however enlightening or 'mutative',[9] that leads to healing, but the patient's response to it. This experience cannot be properly expressed in our ordinary vocabulary. It has to be noted in the successful analysands, felt, attended to and allowed to show itself; it is, moreover, an experience that ranges from being totally pleasing to being severely painful.

Ways of internalization: Active and passive

We could think of two basic modes of internalization: one that seems a natural mechanism, and one that consists of an elaborate process. Of course, when referring to 'active' and 'passive' ways of internalization, we should consider that there are no pure types in the human condition; but then, the effort of discussing our formative vicissitudes perhaps requires that we provisionally make use of distinct types. In the mechanical procedure it is tempting to suggest that the outer object is imploded into the inner system as it is; 'but we know that this is not the case', says Symington.[10] As simply introjected, it results in an inner object that debilitates the self and inhibits spontaneity. There is no neutral introjection – there is either a psychic action that enhances the personality, or a passive introjective mechanism that inhibits it. Once objects are inside our psychic apparatus as a result of a mechanical reaction, it is asserted that this is how they are – or were. They are proclaimed to be what they feel like on the basis of a mechanical imprint, of a mark being imposed.

Active internalization occurs through a manoeuvre of re-creating the object; when we make it ourselves, then we own it inside. We may even end up possessing pain when the outer objects are partially bad and not sufficiently good, but it is a pain with which we do not coincide, and one that we can endure because we do not blindly identify with the objects. This agrees with the general idea that it is the essential creative nature of the mind's life that is sane when it governs mental events, and is ill when it fails to do so. We cannot ignore activity, and so even in receptivity we are active in our receptiveness. But then the question remains whether the outer object, the 'other', which we take to be something to mechanically incorporate, may subsequently become autonomous and may even rule us from within.

Primitive identifications may be thought of in terms of osmosis or contagion – which is indeed a passive approach. Current theorizing makes it possible to anchor early identifications to representations, making early experiences more easily comparable to subsequent ones. There is a gradient in the quality of internalization, from the primitive to the more mature. In parallel, agency and responsibility stand out as being more significant. This resonates well with the Freudian quasi-theory of *Nachträglichkeit*,[11] in the sense that every experience is actively reconstructed and given psychic significance by the subsequent states of maturity and understanding. Without this ongoing reconstructive creativity, there would be no memory, or self. From this same perspective Symington points out one of the unfortunate aspects of some discipleships, such as, for instance, the inhibition of a creative capacity through the process of incorporation of the master. There is often a period of intense submission followed by rebellious detachment that occurs when the disciple tries to dissolve the reciprocal narcissistic bondage. 'The rage towards the erstwhile mentor is the projected hatred of the submissive act. It is the submissive act that is hated, but it becomes projected and hypostasized in the outer object.'[12] This probably means that one can be very sad about not having yet developed one's personal spontaneity. It is even sadder that a former mentor is hated, inasmuch as the hatred is a perverted failure of an attempt at emancipation. True liberation would require that we realize that the enslaving principle is the inner submissive act and also that the enslaving attitude is a typical element of the narcissistic condition.

The unfortunate inclination to incorporate knowledge can even be repeated in the analytic situation in which the analyst can be begged, or seduced, into acting as a divine oracle. No thinking or personal effort is required in the ingestion of enlightened convictions. This may be one of the reasons for seeking to be analysed – or boasting of having been treated – by some prestigious figure. '*Embodiment* of the thoughts of a god has been substituted for thinking.'[13] As is known, dynasties, feuds and schisms within the analytic culture can be seen as indicators of this pervasive human deficit.[14] People fail to be themselves because it is easier to be somebody else and because they can imitate someone else's success rather than risk their own failure. People are in a hurry to magnify themselves by copying what is popular – and are too paralysed or benumbed to think of anything better. We want quick success and are in such a haste to get it that we cannot take time to be true to ourselves. And when the futility of it comes upon us, we argue that our very haste is a sort of 'integrity'. Keeping excessively busy is a way of avoiding being true to oneself, and so the desire to stop being busy meets the aspiration to be true to oneself.

One of the reasons for not feeling spontaneous and for the not uncommon complaint of feeling 'phoney' may point in the direction of an inability to seriously internalize. We may ingest, take in, swallow without any true effort of understanding. We are full of knowledge but not quite knowing, and thus we are sometimes wise enough to complain. In Gaddini's view, it is a very serious manoeuvre of imitation but not quite a metabolic assimilation;[15] it may give a feeling of playing roles – as, for instance, 'psychoanalyst' – but without reaching the joy of spontaneity. This is especially painful in the creative professions, when the lack of spontaneity can induce envy and contentions. But then, the educational system at large puts a prize on information and not on personalized knowledge.

The constant phobia of distress and suffering, together with the desperate search for ever new anaesthetizers, can be regarded as serious impediments to spontaneity. It is paradoxical that learning to suffer well is a precursor to a full psychic life and that the 'act' of suffering can be more enriching than anaesthetized, benumbed indifference. This inconspicuous capacity is the source of psychic strength and health. Following Hesse, we could say that a part of our self – one of our mind-like agents or idols – seems to dictate: 'Pain is just pain, it obviously hurts and no compromise is possible. There are remedies that can defeat frustration and these are weapons that can be produced and successfully used. It would be madness if you would accept suffering.' Another deeper voice, however, may seem to suggest something like this: 'Pain is hurtful only because you fear it so much; it stalks you just because you constantly try to escape it. The most hurtful feature of inner pain is your dislike of it; it is this refusal that makes pain so painful.'[16] Even though the first voice has good reasons on its side, and thus sounds more immediately convincing, we ultimately damage ourselves by producing an incompatibility with pain. The contrast of these two voices can be consuming. The more cogent voice that propels us towards the escape from frustration seems to even profit from the strategies that we use to prevent pain. But then, in a synthetic *aperçu*, we could say that each voice is to some extent – paradoxically – contaminated by the other because both are generated by the very same desire of the other antagonistic voice.

De Monticelli remarks that we may gradually become accustomed to preventing our 'hearts' from being even slightly touched by whatever may be hurtful; we are proficient in the capacity to neutralize experience.[17] Affective acceptance, which is much more than recognition of data and reality, is the exact opposite of neutralizing experience. By being hospitable to potentially threatening contacts, almost to the point of submitting to them, we actually come to see and perceive them: their elimination is not in our power, just as we cannot avoid seeing an object in front of us. But, of course, there is no obligation to keep our eyes open; by not seeing we can behave as if things were not there. The price for all that is loss of insight.

Nowadays we are back to Bion's question of the evasion of pain as an alternative to utilizing it. In fact, the idea that pain – which includes guilt, shame and loss – can be anaesthetized is probably an illusion. Symington insists that there is no anaesthetic, even if we constantly produce new models of it and devise all kinds of arguments to convince ourselves that there is.[18] There is thus a generalized phobia of affliction, as if it were an extinct illness and that it should be shameful to let it reappear. There is no trace of a suggestion that we should get through it because it can ultimately be life enhancing. And if we ask what might be the rightful place for distress, for most people it would be very difficult to accept that there should be any. In his theory of thinking, Bion unequivocally remarks that 'A capacity for tolerating frustration enables the psyche to develop thought as a means by which the frustration that is tolerated is itself made more tolerable.' And he later reiterates that 'People exist who are so intolerant of pain or frustration . . . that they feel the pain but will not suffer it and so cannot be said to discover it.'[19] And it is precisely when one cannot manage to experience pain that one cannot even arrive at the discovery of joy.

Mind-like agents

Gaddini suggests that 'To imitate not only does not mean to introject, but may be a way of defending oneself from the anxiety provoked by intro-jective conflicts, even if the defences may in turn cause more serious pathological conditions.'[20] In fact, when the 'lengthy and laborious' work of internalization is eschewed, we may let into our personality elements that do not lead to self-formation but may only function as mind-like agents. And thus mind-like agents are the result of passive, mechanical, imitative introjections. Each of these (conglomerations of) poorly internalized objects can be a source of action in itself – of mind-like action, but not authentic mental action. And thus the imitatively ingested object (or coalition of objects) is also an internal subject of pseudoaction. 'If one is unaware of that, then confusion is inevitable.'[21] Jung can be credited with advocating a similar outlook when he refers to the function of 'complexes'. In fact, when we endeavour to accomplish something and we feel impeded in the enterprise in spite of our best intentions, 'We are really forced to speak of the tendency of complexes to act as if they were characterized by a certain amount of will-power. When you speak of will-power you naturally ask about the ego. Where then is the ego that belongs to the will-power of the complexes?' Also, 'The so-called unity of consciousness is an illusion. It is really a wish dream. We like to think that we are one; but we are not, most decidedly not. We are not really masters in our house. . . . Complexes are autonomous groups of associations that have a tendency to move by themselves, to live their own life apart from our intentions.'[22] We are not masters in our own house not only because we are sustained and propelled by immense instinctual forces, but also because we may have passively introjected external objects (which were actually subjects, of course) that may coalesce in the form of separate mind-like agents acting on their own. The poorly internalized objects may in turn become constellations, figures or characters. In McDougall's language: 'Whether we will it or not, our inner characters are constantly seeking a stage on which to play out their tragedies and comedies.'[23] And also, 'Language informs us that the scriptwriter is called "I".' But then the 'I' is ruled by these mind-like agents forever craving to reign in the inner stage. 'It is only when we try to re-create everyday scenes upon the psychoanalytic stage that we often discover to our dismay that we are in full performance yet totally ignorant of who the real characters are or what the story is about.'[24] Kernberg remarks that in using the theatre as a metaphor of psychic reality, as a stage for mind-like agents, McDougall hopes to avoid the standard psychiatric and psychoanalytic classification of clinical conditions, which cannot describe anything as complex and subtle as a human personality.[25]

According to Lear, the mind appears as divided into mind-like parts; each part is quasi-rational in itself, and irrationality occurs as a by-product of conflict or interaction between the parts.[26] But then, one of our disquieting problems is that by imitatively ingesting (idealized) objects, these become internal, autonomous epistemic subjects inclined to function as normative agents. These inner ruling figures also come to appear eminently suited to exercise cognitive power, the sort of power that also 'legitimately' produces the sole objects of 'our' concern. From this perspective, the establishment of an impersonal epistemic agency coincides with some normative inner authority legislating on human capacities and areas of 'interest'. This epistemic scenario may inconspicuously asphyxiate any subjective, personal sense of agency. As the inner mind-like agents are the authors of a language that dominates our relational world, we passively use that language as an inconspicuous source of authority in the deceptive equation between authorial and authoritative prerogatives.[27] Under the influence of mind-like agents, we may 'learn' to hold the world away from us and to somehow constitute them as 'superior' epistemic agents through a willed estrangement from it, almost as if the entire venture of knowledge necessarily entailed some form of detachment. It is an estrangement perhaps compensated by the comforting inhabitation of any reigning epistemology. Yet, if we are still sufficiently concerned with our psychic agency, rather than with an abstract rendition of it, we can better perceive that the subjection to mind-like agents is only conducive to a debilitating symbiosis with them.

These mind-like agents cannot enhance authentic relations with other creatures or external values and thus can only sustain a distinctively narcissistic internal policy. The ability to recognize narcissistic currents in our own character is, of course, of great importance. None of us is free from narcissism induced by mind-like agents, and one of the basic aspects of the condition is that it is deeply antagonistic to self-knowledge. We may even indulge in some futile talk about narcissism, but to truly recognize it in ourselves is profoundly distressing. Clinicians are often tempted to observe other creatures from a safe distance and by means of abstract concepts – which is indeed a hubristic game – while never turning their gaze inward to the sources of our intrapersonal vicissitudes. When this demanding passage is avoided, there arises a tendency towards either accusation or futile reassurance. And, of course, analysts also participate in this condition in the sense that they also cope with inner uncoordinated mind-like agents. The failure to recognize autonomous inner agents can be the source of narcissistic confusion for both analyst and patient. These mind-like agents, moreover, work best while being constantly kept in projection – the paramount temptation among clinicians. They defend themselves from recognizing the mad influence of mind-like agents through being closely associated with other subjects who are more obviously disturbed than they are and who can seem to carry the denied aspects of their pathology. It is a liberation when we can realize that we no longer need others to carry our psychotic aspects on our behalf. The inner agents may be so intolerable that each is detached from ourselves and placed in other containers with the illusive hope that they may function out there, like an insufficiently good parent letting the child carry his unbearable parts. 'Without adequate self monitoring' – says Casement – 'an analyst can get into behaving like a pathogenic parent, with all the inevitable consequences.'[28] Only the development of awareness, in the sense that we are cognizant of our own representation of ourselves, can aid in the direction of integrated internal relations.

Integrity of the self could be achieved when virtually all parts of the personality are encircled by creative acts of awareness and acceptance. Once 'all' parts of the self are embraced in this way, the individual is not pressured by the inner agents projected in the social world. Through sufficient awareness we need not expel mind-like parts and need not be impinged by their outside representatives. The challenging features of the mind's life could be summarized by resorting to one of the many ironic and only apparently cryptic remarks by Kierkegaard: 'The self is a relation that relates to itself or is the relation's relating itself to itself in the relation; the self is not a relation but is the relation's relating itself to itself.'[29]

People often come for treatment because of deficiencies in their character that prevent them from managing their lives. These conflicts are experienced as coming in the form of assaults from outside, while probably their origin lies in determinants from within that fashion outer incursions upon the self. Freedom of choice is a core value of modern life, and we tend to believe that we exercise our freedom through the right to choose. We should, however, pose the question whether our supposedly free choices are driven by obedience to hidden agendas emanating from mind-like agents. We of course know how extensively we are conditioned by the well-known 'hidden persuaders' surrounding us. The obscure collusion between mind-like agents and external persuaders makes the problem of spontaneity even more acute. When people use the language of freedom but live in thrall to hidden rules, they place themselves in a dangerous predicament. There is nothing wrong in obeying rules, and there is nothing wrong with exercising free choice. The danger lies in claiming to be doing one thing while actually doing the other. When people claim to be obeying rules but break them, we call this hypocrisy; when people claim to be free but are in fact obeying unstated rules, we do not have a word for it – and there is no word because it is a condition that we are slow to recognize. But we can certainly appreciate that they are not spontaneous. Spontaneity is perhaps developed by being capable of resisting the joint threat of outer persuaders and inner agents.

Mind-like idols

According to the philosopher Francis Bacon, we can aspire to knowledge to the extent that we emancipate ourselves from the blinding idols of our mind (the *Idola*). As is known, he distinguishes four classes of idols: specifically, the 'Idols of the Tribe', the 'Idols of the Cave', 'The Idols of the Forum' and 'The Idols of the Theatre'. The name of the fourth class derives from the notion that rival world views are comparable to stage plays, with different casts and different plots, although all equally fictitious.[30] The philosopher sees their role as preventing the attainment of truth and knowledge. And yet their functioning on a stage makes idealized deities of them, to which we are tempted to submit; like a star-system, the theatre stage is so full of light that we are tempted just to take the idols in as a short cut to a god-like position – the same old, futile trick of just eating a certain apple from the tree of knowledge. And thus I would like to borrow the term 'idol' in order to indicate primitive and blinding aspects of our inner organization. Mind-like idols can be seen as more elusive and constrictive than mind-like agents, more detrimental to the pursuit of spontaneity. Awareness of these elusive but constrictive conditions may create a better quality of clinical preparedness.

The idea of idols may serve to illustrate the consequences of passive imitation as distinct from the results of identification proper. Mind-like idols are thus the result of passive, primitive introjections, which are even more debilitating than mind-like agents. Gaddini says that 'It is fairly widely agreed that imitation reveals itself as a disturbance of identification, and with the characteristics of a primitive phenomenon.'[31] This distinction does not imply that imitation is the opposite of identification, but, rather, that the latter is a more complex phenomenon.

'Idols' can be interpreted as inner pseudo-deities: unattainable, indifferent and tyrannical. To the extent that they are pseudo-gods, they are more like demons intent on impeding knowledge and spreading confusion. As usurpers of divine attributes, idols seem to function as dia-bolic agents in the etymological sense of the word: the Greek term *diaballo* being a compound of the word *dia* ('across') and *ballo* ('I throw'); hence a diabol could be something that flings things across and as a result jumbles them up. If we regard them as mind-like components of our personality, they are indeed more powerful and fearsome than mind-like agents.[32] And so we could endorse Bacon's judicious remark in the paragraph entitled 'Elenchi Magni, sive de *idolis* animi humani natives et adventitiis': 'It must be confessed that it is not possible to divorce ourselves from these fallacies and false appearances, because they are inseparable from our nature and condition of life; so yet nevertheless the caution of them (for . . . all *elenches* . . . are but cautions) doth extremely import the true conduct of human judgement.'[33]

Distress can be due to some awareness of the influence of the pseudo-deities within us. The fear is so great that it is often unbearable. But then, awareness of this distress only arises when the person is no longer terrorized by the idols. Once psychic pain becomes conscious, it is no longer invested with the same terror. Awareness of the panic indicates that the person is much less influenced by it. Paradoxically, part of the inclination to be totally possessed by an idol is that it may alleviate pain. Struggling with awareness necessarily implies that one is not petrified by the idols, that one accepts their presence and thus tries to avoid their influence. In the case of adhesive or symbiotic relations, one is not inhabited by another person but by the mind-like idol displaced by that person. Idols, moreover, are not at all mute, and they dictate on whatever is or is not to be thought in the name of a 'superior' knowledge. It may be remarked here that any form of discourse can be used and ruled by mind-like idols. Aulagnier convincingly argues that the tyranny of discourse is manifested in the abuse that often accompanies it; it is an abuse that, while claiming to serve a superior knowledge, manages to dispossess those against whom it is directed of any possibility of recognizing the violence to which they have been subjected and to transform their most legitimate right to defence into feelings of guilt.[34] Indeed, inner idols that are not recognized as such are ultimately submitted to.

In the enlightening language of Jung we could in fact say that 'we are really forced to see certain inner tendencies, to act as if they were characterized by a certain amount of will power . . . We are hampered by those *little devils* the complexes . . . autonomous groups of associations that have a tendency to move by themselves, to live their own life apart from our intentions.'[35] And thus the idols' dictates strip the person of dignity. Often the command is voiced by others whose voice is felt to issue from a figure invested with supreme authority. Symington points out that, in fact, the case of a person hearing a tyrannical 'voice' is rather the exception.[36] If we call our attention to the simple fact that an object, from its own point of view, is of course a subject, we can appreciate that when objects are passively internalized – imploded, imitated – they determine a coalition of comparable objects which then function as idol-like subjects. He suggests that they could be thought of as minor personalities within the personality which may use the inner world as an object of their domineering behaviour. From Symington's clinical perspective, we could then say that what the analyst meets is not a hatred of the mind-like idols that paralyse the analysand; a figure, institution or ideology outside is hated, ultimately as a displacement of inner idols onto the outer reality.[37] The true object of our hatred is the mind-like idol within – and our submission to it. The idols, moreover, determine an atmosphere of diffused depression, as if we somehow knew that their expulsion into external 'stars' was but a futile solution. The insufficient awareness of our hatred of our mind-like idols causes large parts of the self to be displaced into outer figures, so that they can be worshipped and hated in some other place. And so there can hardly be any spontaneity when much of the personality is imprisoned in outer objects.

When hatred pushes mind-like idols into significant others in the environment, subjects become tranquilly forced into their subservience, and they may become pressured or constrained to the detriment of their potential spontaneity. The attachment to the person who harbours the idol has the quality of adhesive fixity, and the person who has made the projection derives his power and self-esteem from the displaced idol to whom he is bound. The problem, then, is not the presence of mind-like idols per se, but our hostility towards them. Clinical experience also seems to suggest that a mental attitude of acceptance – rather than hatred – might actually alleviate the inner tension. The burden of hostility may then no longer weigh on the subject. Patients often indirectly demand that they be helped to cope with mind-like idols. And it can be in the most unlikely ways – says Casement – 'that we find ourselves getting to where a patient most needs the analysis to reach, if they are to attain release from what has formerly imprisoned them in their minds.'[38] Certain cultural objects are so widely represented as being worthy of idealization that they become the most sought-after containers of our idolic introjects; thus they even soar to the status of normative agents. And yet – according to Silverman – no matter how often it is reiterated, an ideal figure remains a bloodless abstraction until it has been psychically affirmed by our projections.[39] We alone are finally responsible for the production of idolizable ideals. And although it is the subject that has constituted that object as an ideal, he often falls prostrate before it, in thrall to its fascinating lustre. What is especially interesting is that there is a magnetic attraction towards mind-like parts of one's own personality once they are pushed into someone else. They are irremediably attractive because they are home-grown or, still better, are of our own making. In the language of McDougall: 'These delusions . . . are nevertheless lived as an implacable reality by the minds that have invented them.'[40] They are as implacable as primitive deities. And once we feel asphyxiated by this unfortunate condition, we believe that spontaneity can be purchased by destroying the person or institution that has been used for our expulsive purposes – while being constantly on the look-out for still another bearer of idols. The constitutive act of the external idol ultimately establishes it as a pseudo-ethical norm, as a subject tacitly entitled to righteous anger and disdain; these are affects that are, of course, as intense as they are inconspicuous or unidentified. The persecutory nature of inner or outer idols can be experienced when they 'tell' us that we are worthless and nearly instigate us to self-damage. But a reversed perspective of our condition could be truly illuminating: we do not damage ourselves because we are depressed; we actually become depressed because of these disparaging inducements to impair ourselves.

When attempting to reverse our projective propensity because of maturation or disruptions, it feels like having to begin all over again. The quality of rigidity, moreover, is the obscure compulsion to simply comply with the putative way we are and to beware of any inclination to spontaneity. To avoid these straits we even develop philosophies of life that will harmonize with our limits, or else we adhere to ideologies eminently suited to serve our condition of prevented spontaneity, as we have abundantly and repeatedly seen in not so ancient historical events. When the ideology collapses, one is thrown back on oneself, to face one's own mind-like idols and their ultimate viciousness: the tacit obligation to go along in the same way.

Chapter 3

The function of paradox

From splitting to paradox

When trying to explain some clinical turning point or significant maturational event, the most frequently used words are 'paradox', 'paradoxical', 'paradoxically'. These terms, however, are hardly ever contextualized, clarified or defined, and probably for good reason.

By way of introduction we could recall that the word 'paradox' derives from the Greek combination of *para* ('beyond') and *doxa* ('belief'), and so it literally indicates a contention that is incredible – beyond belief. In the etymological sense of the term, paradoxes are thus a matter of far-fetched opinions, peculiar ideals, unbelievable occurrences and such-like anomalies that run counter to ordinary expectations – and yet are quite pertinent to our inner life. In the common usage of everyday discourse, a paradox is a judgement that is contrary to general belief or common sense – and yet is ultimately undeniable. On this basis, according to Rescher, 'A paradox . . . would be an obviously anomalous contention that one seriously propounds despite its conflict with what is generally regarded as true.'[1] If we take the Greek word *'para'* to mean 'against', rather than just 'beyond', then the word comes closer to the meaning of a logical contradiction; in this sense, it means a claim that has an argument to sustain it while being contradictory to logic. Paradox thus appears to be a seemingly sound piece of reasoning based on a seemingly true assumption that leads to a contradiction: an apparently sound proof of an unacceptable conclusion, or an unacceptable conclusion of an apparently sound proof. Formally, a paradox reveals that either the principles of reasoning or the assumptions on which it is based are faulty. In logical disciplines it is said to be solved when the mistaken principles or assumptions are clearly identified and rejected. And also, while philosophically destructive (inasmuch as they arise from problems implicit in the general presuppositions of thought and action), paradoxes are intrinsically fascinating. The problems they pose may prove ultimately to be insoluble, but insight into the origin of paradox can be valued as part of the Socratic ideal of self-knowledge.

In a more personal and non-philosophical usage, a paradox is a statement that seems strikingly implausible, but which in fact conveys an interesting insight. It is in this sense that the witty *bon mots* of celebrated figures may count as paradoxes. And thus, as the classical definitions of the term are primarily philosophical or logical, the concept of paradox is not sufficiently defined in psychoanalysis. In fact, a psychoanalytic paradox is something that strains our minds rather than something that violates logic. And thus the psychological use of the term perhaps indicates the converse, or the other side of paradox – namely the fact that something that seems absurd, inconceivable, incredible turns out to be maturational, beneficial or enlightening. And so we do not have to rectify the assumptions or the principles of reasoning but, on the contrary, appreciate that paradoxical inner vicissitudes are indeed utilizable when the 'wrong' principles or the 'false assumptions' are put to work synergically.

When Freud described transference-love as both real *and* unreal, he was probably trying to describe the unique quality of analytic reality without even trying to make explicit, or acknowledging, the concept of paradox.[2] Modell judiciously suggests that he was actually avoiding an explicitly paradoxical view of the psychoanalytic relationship because he was seeking to establish the scientific status of psychoanalysis within the positivist culture of his times: the recourse to paradox in his descriptions and explanations might have culturally discredited the whole enterprise.[3] And yet, it can be indirectly seen in many of his writings that Freud – the clinician *and* theorist – must have been well aware of the function of paradoxes in psychic life. He possibly steered his attention in the direction of conflict, rather than paradox, in order to prevent being excluded from his current empiricist culture.

The decreasing popularity of psychoanalysis may be due to the increasing recognition that, through the analytic process, there is not much that can be 'obtained', 'acquired' or 'gained'; what is relentlessly attempted, instead, is the development of a capacity to *mentalize* events – to create endurable, paradoxical inner structures that can coexist in our mind. Through this integrative, psychopoietic[4] process we become capable of psychic actions rather than only re-actions. The process may ultimately propose a reversed itinerary: from conflict to paradox, from reactions to actions. When we cannot bear to preserve paradox, we default to its foreclosure and its consequences. Pizer suggests that we then resort to 'segregating-out . . . rigidly bounded, more dissociatively isolated mental constructions. . . . To escape the tensions of holding paradox we tend to categorize reductively, to reify and dichotomize.'[5] In this way we may discard the enrichment of a 'both/and' outlook for the immediate relief of the simpler, and denuding, 'either/or'. The prime casualty of our failure to sustain paradox is our potential for spontaneity: we may be forced to return to the rigidity and monotony of conflict.

The endless process of mentation and self-development can be quite alarming; would it not be better to be and remain numb? In Eigen's view, to have a psyche means to be uncomfortable; any minded sensitive creature is subject to inner pain. Even imagination can function as an infinite source of fear. 'Rage becomes boundless or coagulates into relentless, unforgiving hatred. . . .' If we fulfil one wish, others appear, and there is no end to anticipating dangers, no end to the stream of discontents. It would perhaps be 'safer' not to have a psyche. And Eigen even suggests that 'In one way or another, people try to do just that.'[6]

Pizer also insists that 'Pathology reflects the failure to contain, tolerate, or mediate multiplicity – and thus the degree of dissociation, fragmentation and foreclosure of the internal potential space. Multiple personality can be seen as the failure to communicate between self states, the burning of bridges between islands of psychic reality.'[7] And, in fact, coercing the resolution of a paradox requires the annulment of incongruous self-experiences, the obscuration of conflicts and the ignorance of such mechanisms as projective identification; all this is to preserve the illusion of a 'glassy essence',[8] of a unitary self. But then, there is no suggestion here of a heroic, quasi-ascetic plan of endless maturational growth. We can in fact try wisely to disengage our mind from the obligation to connect and integrate, at least as a temporary measure of appropriate relief; we do need psychic rest. Whether our limitations are natural or cultural, we recurrently note how painful it can be to bear with paradox in our intrapsychic and intersubjective existence. Pizer remarks that 'Paradox perturbs the mind and coerces mental work. And the work of juxtaposing contradictions, encompassing multiplicity and straddling reciprocal negations – while accomplished with the nimbleness of the primary process in our dream world – continually threatens the stable footing of our conscious minds.'[9] That is why even Winnicott, whose acumen envisaged our potential for playing creatively with irresolvable paradoxes, recognized how precariously close the play state is to the brink of 'unthinkable anxiety'.[10]

Kumin points out that 'synthesis', while acknowledging paradox, in fact attempts to dispel it. 'Yet ultimately the experience of paradox can be ego enriching and consoling.'[11] Rosenfeld reiteratively highlights the incomparable pleasure/joy of being able to function well.[12] In a converging perspective on the clinical process, Mitchell suggests that what may be most crucial is neither gratification nor frustration, but the enjoyable process of negotiation itself.[13]

We have so far highlighted the beneficial function of paradox in such a way that it may seem self-defeating not to develop this ego-enhancing capacity. This perspective, however, should not prevent us from recognizing that at severe levels of trauma and inconsistency, paradox becomes unsustainable and the creature deploys the default mechanism of fragmentation. Pizer indicates that in these vicissitudes we essentially perceive the essence of psychic trauma: 'The disruption of the continuity of being.'[14] This disruption derives from the unbearable magnitude of conflict and the degree to which the ego's capacity to develop paradox has become overwhelmed by the shocking juxtapositions; he reasons that perhaps dissociation enters the picture in a gradient, as the capacity to bear and negotiate paradox is increasingly strained towards the breaking point.

Winnicott on paradox

Through his inimitable acumen, Winnicott provides an enlightening presentation of the functions of paradox; in his Introduction to *Playing and Reality* – which was a development of his 1951 paper 'Transitional Objects and Transitional Phenomena' – he says: 'I am drawing attention to the *paradox* involved in the use by the infant of what I have called the transitional object. My contribution is to ask for a *paradox* to be accepted and tolerated and respected, and for it not to be resolved. By flight to split-off intellectual functioning it is possible to resolve the *paradox*, but the price of this is the loss of the value of the *paradox* itself. The *paradox* . . . has value for every . . . individual who is not only alive . . . but who is also capable of being infinitely enriched by the exploitation of the cultural link with the past and with the future.'[15] It may be noted that with total disregard of style, in this brief passage Winnicott uses the term 'paradox' *five* times, as if he were somehow striving to infuse its value into the reader; it is a quasi-performative rather than merely informative statement. This introduction is, in fact, a renewed perception of his work of twenty years before. It may also be noted that we see here a lively example of the capacity for what is variously referred to as '*Nachträglichkeit*', 'deferred effect', 'retranscription of memory', 'recategorization of experience', 'retrospective attribution' or '*après coup*'. He in fact reinterprets his work in the light of his greater awareness of the function of paradox. For indeed, in his brief Introduction he tries to forcefully communicate that the capacity of paradox is essential to the development of subjective agency – of spontaneity. Inasmuch as they attempt to actively connect self and objects, transitional phenomena that enhance the growth of subjectivity can thus be regarded as the precursors of paradox in the sense of an effort to link diverging elements.

   Eigen emphasizes that 'for Bion the ultimate reality of the self is beyond the reach of knowledge. However, openness to the unknown is *the* formal and essential working principle by which psychoanalysis must proceed.'[16] The whole enterprise of analysis is a 'play' whereby we attempt a confrontation with the unknown. As is well known, we need the famous 'good-enough parent' in order to develop into adults, but we also need the capacity to deal with the partially bad parent which can never be eliminated from experience. The question is how it is possible to manage that part of the good-enough caretaker that does not nourish but instead intoxicates; this bad part we must accept along with any good nourishment. The capacity to keep 'together' these apparently incompatible elements is that unknown inner force that we seek to understand. The incapacity to manage poisonous and nourishing experiences may involve the renunciation of otherness and a default towards narcissism. Ideally this 'filtering' function – which is not quite a mental filter – is provided by the capacity to treat conflict in the form of paradox: contradictions may be lived as negotiations, and oppositions as modes of differentiation. This is a challenge, a 'play' that is both creatively playful and extremely serious.

At this point it is perhaps appropriate to just indicate some brief *aperçus* of paradox without any attempt to hierarchize or coordinate them. Simone Weil, for instance, reiterates that 'We cannot imagine the joy of spontaneity when it is absent, thus the incentive for seeking it is lacking.'[17] How is that for a paradox? As a result of coping with such heterogeneous experiences as ruthlessness and concern, privacy and connectedness, separateness and interrelatedness, dependency and autonomy, destructiveness and creativity, envy and guilt, destruction and reparation, we may need some kind of restful pause. Winnicott's transitionality can be seen as a 'resting-place for the individual engaged in the perpetual human task of keeping inner and outer reality separate yet interrelated'.[18] But is not transitionality a demanding achievement? It is indeed a peculiar and paradoxical 'resting-place'.

Parsons claims that play is at work all the time in psychoanalysis within a frame where things can be real and not real at the same time. This paradoxical setting is what allows the work of analysis to take place.[19] And then, when the 'play at work' is not possible, the analyst's effort 'is directed towards bringing the patient from a state of not being able to play into a state of being able to play'.[20] That is, to resist in paradox and bear with it; in fact, a doll must be both a toy and a baby.

Rayner says that 'a child may lie on the beach lapped by the waves and exclaim "I am a stone". As he is playing he knows he is not a stone, but the point of the game is that he *is* a stone. Without symmetry there is no play, but without asymmetrical logic, play breaks down into delusion, he *believes* he is a stone.'[21] It is indeed an ongoing oscillation between symmetrical and asymmetrical mental levels.

In the light of Symington's outlook, we could say that it is the 'option' that creates the 'other'. And yet the problem is that others have their own independent existence. And so the paradox is that the other has an independent existence but 'does not exist without being opted for'.[22]

Parsons remarks that whenever the infant pretends to be feeding a grown-up, 'The feeding can be treated as real provided it is not really treated as real. If that does happen, it stops being real at all.'[23]

Eigen points out that a child may feel put down by parents, yet may also feel loved by them. How could he love them if they were bad? How could he hate them if they were good to him? In his view, 'ultimately one never knows whether one is hating or loving the good or the bad parent'.[24] These are paradoxical doubts, indeed.

Pizer emphasizes that there is a 'tension in living between the fresh potentials of the present moment and enmeshment in the conservative grip of repetition of our past experience'.[25] And yet the capacity for consistent repetition is life-supportive; if not, how could we possibly stabilize our maturational steps? Still another paradox.

As is known, Bion maintains that the infant is connected to outer figures for reasons of survival and thus, however frustrating it may be, he cannot entirely forswear them – but he can detest them. Symington points out that the frustrated child turns inward to the phantasmal bad figures, with the consequence that he will strive to make outer good figures conform to his negative inner images; he thus manipulates them into this imposed role. But they can still remain good, and 'When an outer figure resists this powerful projective pressure, the individual bursts out with rage.'[26] How is that for a clinical paradox?

Conflict and paradox

The basic hypothesis is that while conflict induces psychic reactions (rather than actions), tolerated paradox is the condition for proper actions. In Rescher's view, conflict arises as the product of cognitive overcommitment – that is, as the consequence of an excessive attribution of meaning-value – and an overload of sense.[27] However severe, conflicts do not strain or violate our 'logic'.[28] Conflicts may strain our resources, patience or endurance, but not our profound rationality. We can fairly easily become capable of enduring a conflict inasmuch as our mind can redirect attention from one side to the other; we can mentally visualize a conflict and also resort to common logic and think: If this, then either this or that. But then the heavier burden of psychic paradox may be seen to lie in the 'violation' of the 'excluded middle', in the sense that a proposition can be both true and false at the same time. In the psychological writings of his maturity, Wittgenstein appropriately draws attention to the distinction between 'logical impossibility and psychological impossibility'.[29]

There is a specific contribution given by caretakers towards the infant's development of the affect accompanying the mastery of paradox; this is the shared feeling that existence of the impossible is acceptable, even if it strains the accommodating capacity of our minds. Conflicts do not strain the mind in the same way and to the same extent; they in fact indicate oppositional interests between persons or between tendencies within the self. According to Pizer, paradox instead connotes 'the simultaneous coexistence of mental contents or parts of the self that reciprocally contradict each other. Paradox cannot be resolved in that mutually negating elements continue to coexist yielding not resolution but the capacity of straddling contradictory perspectives.'[30] In practical conflicts we can more easily afford to be flexible and pragmatic because the possibility of a compromise is in view. But, for the gifted, intelligent beings that we are, intangible matters of truth are something else, for in fact it is by means of the attribution of truth values that we clearly differentiate attitudes that are prescribed from attitudes that are ultimately proscribed.[31] (As far as *knowledge* is concerned, falsehoods must be demonized, but as far as conflictual *practice* is concerned, the matter is otherwise.)

A distinction between conflict and paradox induces us to accept the essential questions of our human condition more easily. How can we engage in conflicting/contradicting accounts of experience? How could conflicting interpretations be epistemically demarcated and yet be reasonably managed? When there are conflicts, how can opponents remain open and understand enough to negotiate? Is there a way towards negotiation with the most acute of tensions? Pizer points out that parties negotiate not because they are in conflict, but because they are in a condition of both conflict and interdependence. Negotiation of conflictual interests will begin only when each party tacitly or explicitly recognizes some area of overlapping interests. The interdependence of conflicting parties and the search for an area of overlap that coexists with opposition constitute the common point of departure for most negotiation theorists.[32] Of course, we attempt to appreciate the greater maturational value of paradox ('both/and' thinking) with respect to conflict ('either/or' thinking). We should nevertheless recognize and affirm the presence of important conflicts in our mind's life. But then, what should be avoided at all costs is the replacement of potentially creative paradoxes with simple conflicts. Because paradox may strain the mind to the breaking point, we might resort to thinking about paradox as if it were a conflict. Paradox that is not restricted and illusorily reduced to a conflict opens a potential space for integrative and innovative subjective action; this is the capacity for initiative, intentionality, forgiveness, acquittal and imagination. As an alternative to creative, self-formative functioning, we could only determine an inner scenario of passivity. Rosenfeld insists on the unique pleasure/joy of good inner functioning and of the bitter sadness of defensive psychic rigidity.[33] The more passive we become, the more we determine a deadening style of inner life.

From a synoptic view, we could say that a conflict is more easily endurable because we can see the parts of it as circumscribed conglomerations; a paradox is more difficult to sustain because the contending oppositions converge in our thinking. Conflict can be understood; paradox can be only explored. Once we conceptualize in terms of conflict, in fact, we organize our thought into dichotomous categories; a polarity is thus established that seems to require the privileging of one or the other pole – and their reciprocal exclusion. Conflict designates the 'either/or' opposition of contents that is obtained when the 'both/and' creative tension of paradox has collapsed. When confronting a conflict, we can easily choose to vote and envisage a condition of losers and winners. But then, as in the massive rituals of human conflicts, there is only massive loss on both sides. In facing a conflict we can easily engage in splits and projections. A paradox is created when we manage to accept that two contrasting experiences are indivisible and ineliminable.

In Pizer's view, the Oedipal story carries the tragic implications of a failure in the family to negotiate the multiple, contradictory promptings experienced at the core of each individual. The negotiation of paradox in the family matrix elementally contains the dilemmas that are faced at every level of experience when existential paradoxes cannot be endured and 'are collapsed, concretized into tribal conflicts, where splitting mechanisms and discriminatory arrangements remove the disquieting internal tensions incumbent in each individual's concurrent promptings both to separate from and to join the Other'.[34]

The challenge of integration

Integration lies in our continuously renewed capacity for negotiating ever new paradoxes within the self as well as between self and others: in the language of Pizer, 'Thus, psychic life can be viewed as the mind's integrative process, yet not an integration; a bridging process, but not a bridge.'[35]

We should also consider that integration is no synthesis. Tolerating ambivalence, being able to feel both love and hate towards the same object, does not imply that love and hate are synthesized in such a way that hopefully love triumphs over hate. It rather means that hatred can be borne.[36] Discrepancies, conflicts and hiatuses can be surmounted not so much because the self becomes ideally unified, but because being divided comes to be tolerated. The inclusion of segregated affects or blocked aspirations is motivated not by an omnipotent compulsion to restore unity, but out of the desire to be less resentful and fearful of projected anger, less terrified of loss, less punitive towards our dreams. Integration does not imply a fictional Cartesian unity but, rather, the growing ability to benevolently call those voices 'I', and not to disidentify with any one of them. The ability to disidentify is decisive for the reflexive process that makes ideals and identities separable and adaptable rather than compulsory and coercive. As is known, conflict may (or may not) be resolved through choice, action, power or compromise. Paradox, conversely, is the contradictory multiplicity that we dare to reconnect in managing our subjective life: while it requires – and indeed enforces – negotiation, it guarantees no final unity.[37] In fact, it is not easy to hold emotionally to the evidence of good and bad qualities inhabiting the same person. And then, we cannot simply say of a creature that he is both greedy and generous, intrusive and welcoming, for we should perhaps more accurately say that an individual can be greedy but generous, intrusive but welcoming, in the sense that these contrasting qualities do not simply go together but almost seem to function as paradoxical co-agents in spite of each other.[38] This is an attempt to utilize the acumen that is required for these essential assessments. In his philosophy of psychology, Wittgenstein judiciously remarks that 'We are playing with . . . flexible concepts. But this does not mean that they can be deformed *at will* and without offering resistance . . .'.[39]

We constantly endeavour to bear with paradoxes while maintaining a sense of unruptured continuity of the self. At primitive levels of offence and incongruence, paradox becomes unsustainable and we make a coerced return to conflict and fragmentation.[40] The development of integration depends on the relative severity of conflicts *and* on the degree to which the propensity of the self to connect elements and develop paradox may become overburdened by traumatic, discrepant combinations. There is perhaps a gradient in the tolerability of paradoxes. As a result of conflicts of extreme severity, some of the more daring paradoxes developed to face the challenge cannot ultimately be tolerated. The strain to psychically elaborate 'enormous' paradoxes may impose an excessive burden on the mind's affective life. In fact, we can occasionally disengage our mind from the 'obligation' to create mental connections and bridges as a way of creating a temporary relief, a restful pause. Winnicott says that 'Relaxation for an infant means not feeling a need to integrate.' But then he has to add that this relaxation is only possible when the 'the mother's ego-supportive function . . . [is] taken for granted'.[41]

From the perspective of self-integration, we can easily recognize that we constantly try to nourish each other, and continue to do so. And yet we can also recognize that our nourishing efforts convey a varying dose of psychic poison.[42] It should be noted that, in the analytic itinerary, we come to observe that accepting this recognition brings us to psychic connections we could not otherwise have reached.

As a complement to the concept of paradox, we could use the idea of 'cycles' as a way towards our mind's integration; or we could even look at paradox as if it were some kind of psychic metabolic cycle. Thibon suggests that struggling to transform a situation in such a way that it will be entirely good is definitely obfuscating. Some kind of cycle should instead be envisaged, such as being understood in order to understand, working in order to eat, eating in order to work: 'If we regard one of the two as an end, or the one and the other taken separately, we are lost. Only the cycle contains the truth.'[43] Thus, integration could even be seen as an ongoing cycle. If we need things to be entirely good for our mental survival, then we become actually convinced that 'revolution' is needed, as if we were saying to ourselves, 'Just wait until things finally change and then all will be fine within me.' But this 'revolutionary' outlook could indeed come to function as 'the opium of the people'.

The problem of integration does not only pertain to the individual or to the human condition, as can be intuitively conceded. The problem also seems to exist in the epistemology of the empirical sciences. It is instructive and consoling to see it at work there; this enlightening limitation can be illustrated through Feinman's remarks to the effect that 'the statements of science are not of what is true and what is not true, but statements of what is known to different degrees of certainty: "It is very much more likely that so and so is true than that it is not true"; or "Such and such is almost certain but there is still a little bit of doubt"; or – at the other extreme – "Well, we really don't know". Every one of the concepts of science is on a scale graduated somewhere between absolute falsity or absolute truth. . . . It is of great value that when we make decisions in our life, we don't necessarily know that we are making them correctly; we only think we are doing the best we can – and this is what we should do.'[44]

Chapter 4

Subjective agency – *and* passivity

In search of subjective agency

Psychoanalytic literature seems to generally convey a principle of inherent subjective agency that is never explicitly theorized, while it is also constantly presupposed. It is therefore necessary to be aware of these interlocking attitudes if we are to make the best use of our psychoanalytic tradition. And so, in our ongoing reflections we should be on the look-out for hints of subjective agency – both theories and assumptions – as well as intent upon the detection of psychic passivity. Most authors, in fact, do not explicitly recognize a 'germ' of subjective agency, but they do use this assumption all along in their writings.

Bion, for instance, refers to an 'alpha function' to indicate that human potential which is the provenance of thinking.[1] The sense of his contribution is that it is appropriate for us to assume that there is a psychic locus – a force – from which creative acts of connection issue forth. We could tentatively say that there are two alternative conditions in inner life: one where there is a state of uncoordinated fragments, and one in which an organizing, creative principle is at work. This general perspective is clearly implied in Freud's remarks to the effect that the patient presents us with a torn mind; but some agentive, creative part must be at work for, in fact, 'The psycho-synthesis is achieved during analytic treatment *without* our intervention.'[2] And similarly: 'An activity without ownership requires as its counterpart a *perverse form of passivity*.'[3] From a psychoanalytic perspective, we could then differentiate personal mental action from impersonal mental behaviour. Personal action is the metabolic act of a principle of integration, whereas impersonal behaviour is ultimately a sequence of reactions.

From a therapeutic perspective, what is transformative is creative psychic action. Interpretation per se does not bring about the change. 'Interpretation', writes Symington, 'may . . . encourage the individual towards the moment of psychic action . . . [but] the inner psychic action is made by the person alone.'[4] You can create conditions that facilitate the creative step, but you cannot actually make the step for the other person; this psychic action has to occur from within. Pathology, moreover, could be said to derive not only from an undeveloped potential for personal action, but also from some 'blind' resistance to it. A comparable outlook is presented by Tustin where she remarks that 'The difference between normal and pathological autism is one of degree rather than kind. It might be said that pathological autism is a state of anti-thinking.'[5] If we could draw a parallel with this enlightening distinction, we could say that a benign situation could be described in terms of pre-agency, whereas a more malignant inclination could be understood in terms of anti-agency. A comparable point is made by Kristeva: 'Because of your soul, you are capable of action. Your psychic life is a discourse that acts. Whether it harms you or saves you, you are its subject.'[6] In the essay entitled 'Creative Activity and the Search for the Self', Winnicott reiterates that a paradox is involved in his theory, 'which *needs* to be accepted, tolerated, and not resolved'.[7] He appears to recognize that self-formation can only be conceptualized if we allow for some inchoate capacity to actually develop and think paradoxical connections. He seems to suggest that every seminal theory or proto-model presupposes some kernel of inherent subjectivity. While constantly bearing in mind the indispensable function of the facilitating environment, he suggests, however, that the development of the infant is not entirely and causally dependent on good-enough parenting.[8] Simone Weil reports Thucydides as saying that 'By a necessity of nature every being invariably exercises all the power of which it is capable'[9] – possibly implying that a source of psychic power is presupposed. From this same view, Symington contends that 'What leads to psychic change is inner psychic action. Interpretation [alone] does not bring about change. . . . It is essential to reach the real good, the spontaneous action within a person and to give that our full support.'[10]

But then, this so often implied originary 'germ' of thinking cannot be equated with an autonomous, coherent rational 'I'. This deceptive Cartesian view serves to deny the subjacent or supervenient 'reality' of a fragile, vulnerable Ego, whose *active* efforts to internalize and develop meaning may be basically defensive.[11] And yet the advocacy of meaning over chaos, integration over fragmentation, thinking over symptom, consciousness over unconsciousness remain essential to psychoanalysis. And so if this principle of inherent subjective agency is constantly presupposed, but never explicitly theorized, we should perhaps infer that from its start the theoretical background of psychoanalysis is not entirely coherent.

There are some things in our personality that are important, and a good many that are not. It does not take too much discrimination to work out which are which. Being psychically active is one. The critique of identity, moreover, does not prevent us from positing a psychic subjectivity that takes up various positions through identification; a kind of 'identifier behind the identification', in the language of Benjamin.[12] Humans can be regarded as a composite of determination and agency, and of course there are areas where one predominates with respect to the other. What frequently happens, however, is a 'political' attempt to categorize all of human behaviour under one rubric or other. Symington contends that the idea of intertwinement that seems to run through the whole of human activity to a greater or lesser extent should constantly be respected and deferred to.[13] The delicate but essential point in the exploration of constriction and spontaneity is that it is not primarily a question of prevalence in the mixture of the two different components but, rather, a question of option, response, acceptance or refusal of something; it is a realization that at certain turns we cannot be travelling in two different directions. And yet, our life journey should not be conceived as travelling by air or train – in the sense that our destination cannot be changed – but more like an itinerary on foot in which at every step we can redefine the destination, route and pace.

In common parlance, we metaphorically refer to something as 'dead' when it lacks goal-directed behaviour, initiative or the capacity to function creatively. Conversely, we say that someone is lively and spirited when we recognize the ability to create a valuational perspective and to envisage a move. Even ancient patterns of human coexistence were quite useful, we could say; most people, with rare exceptions, fit themselves into the assigned roles and routines that somehow gave them an inner life of emotions. Only a small fraction of humanity created new roles or circumvented existing roles. Perhaps people find now that they have a mind's affective life that is far more complex than accepted roles either demand or offer. Life is difficult, and perhaps we should be 'grateful' that it is so; if it were not, we would not grow, or learn to change, or have a chance to rise above ourselves.[14] If we just dream, life may whiz past us and we will miss it. If, on the other hand, we can dedicate ourselves to areas where we can make some difference, then inner life becomes richer. We are more, or less, sane human beings on account of how we let constrictions and traumas affect us; it is how we let them affect us that is the critical element. Perhaps some minimal, authentic agency helps the individual to 'use' frustrations in the sense that they can motivate the self rather than damage it. But then, this minimal shift in perspective would induce the analysand – person, subject – to make an inner transition from a prevalent sense of passivity, or desire for compensation, to an outlook of creativity, however minimal. This is a basic confrontation in analysis, and it involves the discovery of the deadening patterns that in total obscurity prevent transition moves from passivity to creativity. The invisible saboteur seems to have the power of gravity in the constant insinuation that we have been *too* badly affected to even think of some personal creativity. Even 'just' entering analysis involves some sort of intentional plan. If the subject does not plan his plan, it may remain a dream. The question is whether we can posit some inner principle of subjective agency that is capable of valuation and orientation; if this principle cannot be posited, then we somehow induce ourselves to proclaim that we are irremediably determined by the interlocking influence of our nature/ nurture constraints.

The inner possibility of valuation which helps to tolerate frustrations is the activity that is at the heart of sanity. A contingency that is tolerated is contained rather than expelled. Symington reiterates that 'the nature of the object is determined by the emotional activity in relation to it'.[15] For instance, one might believe that parents are jealous and tyrannical and that they have been neglectful and abusive since one's early days. One may believe that they did not want their child to develop into a creative adult, and that these are the reasons for the current unfortunate condition. Symington suggests that this not so uncommon complaint can be considered as an unhealthy view, not because parents were not so obnoxious – perhaps they really were – and not because they did not want their child to develop well – perhaps they in fact did not. It is unhealthy because the subject seems to have excessively consented to their perverse wishes. And, moreover, the subject hates to have to endure his hatred of them. The disturbing problem is the feeling of not being a sufficiently lively responder within.[16] This inner consent is the subjective reaction that distorts perception. It is not, perhaps, a perception of the caretakers that is hated, but one's submission to them. It is one's passivity that is ultimately resented. The response is not to the caretakers but to the relationship with them, which is erroneously considered a perennial, binding relation. In fact, the healthy subjective responder within will have considered it exasperating but not really binding.

We commonly say that the self retreats into itself because of insufficiently good caretakers, unable to properly adapt to their infants – a retreat, or implosion, that takes place because they encounter an emotional vacuum in the adults. The extreme rendition of this vacuum is offered by the experiment of the 'enlightened' monarch Frederick II of Sicily. A thirteenth-century chronicle by Salimbene de Adam of Parma narrates how the king wished to find out which had been the first language ever spoken on earth, wondering whether it had been Hebrew, Greek or Latin. The scientifically inclined sovereign arranged for a number of new-born children to be kept in isolation, with the injunction that they be seen only for feeding purposes and that no one should ever talk to them. He had worked out that the language that the secluded infants would spontaneously begin to speak would be the first language that had ever existed on earth. The result of the experiment is unknown, as not one of the children survived. And Salimbene remarks: 'How could they have survived without the cuddles, gestures, smiles and endearments of their nurses?'[17] This tragic historical example is invoked as a way of pointing to the extreme end of the gradient of insufficiently good parenting. But if we move along the scale in the direction of sufficiently good care, we may more beneficially use analysis by also considering the *problem* of insufficiently active responses. This very elusive but crucial difficulty may be totally ignored in a collusive blindness of both analyst and analysand; the effort to make it conspicuous, explicit and sayable may significantly enhance the efficacy of treatment.

We could say that the impersonal, 'outsourcing' management of affective difficulties probably accounts for the absorption and use of most of our world resources. Whether we seek antidotes for our fear of death or fear of loneliness, for the fear of losing physical territories or epistemic spaces, there is always the immense actual cost of ministering to these affects – enormous costs that are still perplexingly ignored. Whenever we are ensnared in repetitive, perverse mechanisms of seeking remedies and compensations, we silently succumb to a sense of passivity that is as severe as it is pervasive. We seem to know of everything, but there is nothing we can do about it. This diffuse passivity can be silently interwoven with any sorts of language games (or *jeux de massacre*) and forms of life (or ways to extinction).

The affliction of passivity

Increasing degrees of passivity may incline towards a deadening condition of inertness, rigidity, perhaps only conducive to attempting futile, parasitic 'relations'. Vulnerable to obscurity because of insufficient reflection, the affliction of passivity is as elusive as it is damaging. As a basic human problem, it is clinically essential and culturally urgent.

We could think of passivity as characterized by an effacement of all differences – between just and unjust, life and death, beautiful and shoddy – as an annulment of the possibility of differentiation that is not contingent but pervasive. We shall thus try to approach this problem from different perspectives.

Major literature has frequently illuminated the ineffable tragedy of passivity. In Dante's *Comedy*, for example, we can perhaps encounter one of the most revealing instantiations of this dangerous affliction. De Monticelli suggests that this condition could be called 'the blinding gaze of the Gorgon'.[18] Dante shows us his pilgrim in the lower world in a state of mortal danger, not so much upon reaching the lowest point of the Inferno – from which he will come out into the world of life – but long before that. The prospect of mortal danger is, in fact, the approaching but avoided encounter with the Gorgon – the mythical, snake-haired, feminine being who petrifies beholders. This ultimate danger is circumvented by the rational guidance – and actual manual intervention – of Virgil: he explicitly tells Dante to turn backwards and to keep his eyes closed because if he met the Gorgon's gaze all chances of ever coming out of the Inferno would be lost.

'Turn thee backwards, and keep thy eyes closed:
for if Gorgon shew herself, and thou shouldst
see her, there would be no returning up again.'
Thus said the Master, and he himself turned me,
and trusted not my hands, but closed me
also with his own.

And then, with specific reference to mental sanity, Dante urges:

O ye, who have sane intellects, mark the
doctrine, which conceals itself beneath the
veil of the strange verses![19]

In a way, Milton's exploration of 'evil' is less radical than Dante's;
Milton, in fact, presents a more reassuring view of wickedness in the sense
that the distinction of good and evil is maintained and that malignancy is
nothing but the hatred of 'good'. We may thus realize that the passivity of
benumbment cannot simply be qualified as obscurity and error since it
actually gravitates towards the lack of any distinction, where no differentiation between 'good' and 'evil' may be vouched for. This distinction holds
as long as even the slightest choice can be made between them. And the first
elements to fall in the torpor of passivity are the functions of choice,
distinction and differentiation.[20]

As a further way of exploring the damages of passivity, we could say that
it can commonly manifest itself in the absence of all hostility and personal
hatred; it appears rooted in that specific absence of sentience which we call
indifference, in the sense of a condition of psychic deadness.[21] The definition that Arendt applies to the case of an executive of the Nazi regime is
'the banality of evil'; this expression could be translated into 'the imper-
sonality of evil'.[22] The damaging affliction of passivity is elaborated by
Benjamin, especially where she points out that 'An activity *without
ownership* requires as its counterpart a perverse form of passivity.'[23]

The puzzling aspect of the paradigm case presented by Arendt is the
inner emptiness of the subject, and the incapacity to feel any difference
between his role and his crimes. Even in less conspicuous cases it is not a
question of cognitive defects but of an extinguished affective life. And so
the origin of hatred might ultimately be thought of in terms of indifference,
as if the foundation of hatred were an absence or a deficiency. In the words
of De Monticelli: 'Imperscrutable as the darkest obscurity, indifference is
the very shadow of hatred, its de-spirited and dispiriting essence, or rather
nothingness.'[24]

But then, could we suggest that cases of extreme psychic passivity can be
said to be the product of despair? Not quite. With his inimitable acumen,
Kierkegaard points out that despair is self-defeating and there is nothing it

can produce, not even a state of radical passivity. In his only apparently cryptic language he says: 'Despair is veritably self-consuming, but an impotent self-consuming that cannot do what it wants to do. What it wants to do is to consume itself, something it cannot do, and this impotence is a new form of self-consuming, in which despair is once again unable to do what it wants to do, to consume itself.'[25]

If we now enter a more clinical perspective, we can agree with Symington that, paradoxically, 'In the person who is most passive, most jelly-like, there is at the same time the most virulent projective identification. . . . It is very common for someone who is very passive to be surrounded by people who are exasperated with him.'[26] A crucial factor in the narcissistic passive subject is the absence of an emotionally creative centre. This deficiency forces the individual into adhesive attitudes in the attempt to seek a centre of action in the other person, and thus avoid the burden of spontaneity and freedom.

The effect of an action will depend on its source. Sometimes quite a small action can generate a considerable rage. 'I was just trying to . . .', we often say. 'Just' is the revealing word: it is supposed to mean that the action had no source, that the agent is totally inert, passive, thing-like – and that the offence just *happened*. According to Symington, 'When you are divorced from the source, then you cannot know it. Remember, the narcissist must not know; he will live for a long time, as long as he does not know himself. Disconnection is essential.'[27] From this same perspective, but more confidently, Schaefer points out that 'Interpretation brings home to the analyzand the extent to which, and the terms in which, the analyzand has been the author of his or her own life, unconsciously and preconsciously as well as consciously; at the same time it brings home the extent to which, and the terms in which, the analyzand has been disclaiming this activity.'[28]

In her exploration of the new maladies of the soul, Kristeva claims that there are individuals whose colourless discourse betrays enormous suffering. 'They speak of their suffering by confiding various stories in the "operative" and "technical" fashion that is typical of those afflicted with psychosomatic illnesses. They then dispose of these stories as if they were lifeless objects or waste products.'[29] Even the analyst may be at once appealed to *and* rejected, called upon *and* closed out, coerced in the futile effort of producing health without any active participation on the part of the analysand. Whatever the differences in the contemporary 'maladies of the soul', they seem to share a common denominator of passivity, as if insight were an unbearable effort and stupor were preferable.

To varying degrees of severity, no one is immune from the affliction of passivity. Even psychoanalysts and their professionality may be endangered by passivity. In the work entitled *Open Minded*, Lear says that his 'book is above all a response to a sense of *deadness*'.[30] And he also wonders whether it isn't the point of all professions to instil deadness. 'Of course the conscious self-image of every profession is that it is there to maintain high standards. And there must be *some* truth in this image. But what does this image cover over? Don't standards themselves impose a kind of rigidity on a practice?'[31] That is, this attitude enables a profession to stop thinking critically about how it ought to go on precisely because the standards present themselves as having already answered the question. The profession can then act as though it *already knows* what high standards are. And Lear concludes, 'This is a form of deadness.'[32] But psychoanalysis is an activity that resists professionalization rather well and recognizes in fact that any set of norms presents itself as having already-answered questions. Whatever other functions they may have, norms often serve as a defence against living openly with the fundamental questions of one's profession – ultimately, a possible evasion of life. According to Lear, 'This is why, for Socrates, the unexamined life is not worth living: it is not a form of living but a form of deadness.'[33] To live openly with the fundamental questions is to avoid assuming that there are any fixed answers that are already given. This is above all an avoidance of all forms of 'knowingness'.[34]

The question then is whether we can regain some spontaneity and freedom from the compulsion of our inner 'norms', in the sense of seeking ever-new ways of coping with life. In this outlook, we may sometimes even have to reverse our perspectives. We may perhaps have to reverse questions and ask whether the subject 'wishes' to harm himself because he is depressed or whether he is depressed because his deadening style of life tends to make him stifled, passive, inert. The latter question may be of greater aid in exploring the affliction of passivity.

In Eigen's view, individuals seek therapy when cumulative toxins threaten to overwhelm their sense of aliveness.[35] At one pole there are creatures who perceive the danger and seek help to negotiate it. They are aware that deadening tendencies in themselves may lead to fatal miscalculations. At the other end, individuals may be so 'poisoned' that they subside to a condition of passive torpor. He eloquently remarks that 'Good elements are infiltrated by a toxic atmosphere that seems inescapable. These individuals may feel basically marred or crippled and succumb to depressive inertia or masochistic fatigue. They are entombed in worthlessness and feel . . . played by something inexplicable that works against them.'[36]

In still another outlook on passivity we could say, with Bollas, that it can take the form of a parody of life.[37] Intriguingly, it may even be the case that individuals develop obsessions and preoccupations as transformations of a desperate state of passivity. He claims that 'the envy of the self that could have been, but will not be, can lead to a form of indifference, or a masochistic celebration of life's conventions that would appear to be evidence of adaptive creativity but that in truth is an attack on the self through a too-rigorous embrace of the necessary devotions of a lifetime. Thus, finding a passionate interest in *one* phenomenon at the exclusion of all others can in certain circumstances be a compromise formation between total restriction and the freedom to develop.'[38] In such instances, passivity comes to be transformed into a travesty or caricature of life.

Initiative and intentionality: Psychic birth

The process of enhancing initiative and intentionality can be conceived in terms of maieutics: the art of midwifery transferred into the domain of psychology.[39] As a uniquely non-directive form of therapy, psychoanalysis may be regarded as a procedure of assistance to the birth of the analysand's more authentic self; it is a way of assisting the effort of being born – provided that some vital part of the personality, however minimal, is there eagerly seeking to be born, to accept the challenging gift of psychic life. Seeking to be born into psychic life without any form of assistance may at times be experienced as too demanding. Maieutics is a prerequisite of interpretation in the sense of helping the healthier part of the self to spring to life, to become real and living, notwithstanding reluctances and difficulties. Only through being born may one feel real and living. Eigen points out that for Winnicott, 'The essential battle is over one's sense of realness: does one feel real to oneself or merely a phantom or splinter self?'[40] Initiative and intentionality are indispensable features of one's sense of realness; he also claims that Bion, Winnicott and Lacan systematically attempted 'to take up the problem of ideal experiencing in its own right, as a spontaneously unfolding human capacity related to existential concerns'.[41]

Both actions and reactions are customarily attributed to the 'I' of the inner world. But it is only the spontaneous 'I' that has the capacity for initiative and intentionality; that these are desirable it is easy for us to see, but the reasons why they are also fearsome are not so obvious. We constantly talk of self-formation but hardly ever of the necessity of self-decreation for the sake of psychic birth. Once initiative and intentionality are perceived as truly personal, they have to be felt and accepted as the challenging gift of psychic life. The emergence of any spontaneity, however, seems to involve a sense of panic and bewilderment, as if one were facing major losses, when in fact it is an irreversible transition from a more natural and biological condition to a more dialogic, symbolic and challenging existence.[42] But then, there is also something of a virtuous circle to it in the sense that intentional, personal action 'reveals' the self and ultimately facilitates its own birth. The desire to be born. Birth itself is not quite a reversible experience; it implies the acceptance of the challenge of inner life and is the last thing we would forswear once we have entered the process of mental development.

If we ideally consider the 'I' of the personality to be the unifying centre and source of creative action, we could subscribe to Winnicott's suggestion that 'Before a certain era . . . only a very few people lived creatively. . . . To explain this one would have to say that before a certain date it is possible that there was only very exceptionally a man or a woman who achieved *unit status* in personal development.'[43] This 'unit status' might be regarded as an image or precursor of the Bionian idea of the thing in itself, in its ultimate reality – for which he uses the sign 'O'. And this designation is not only developed to explore the outer world of persons and things, but also one's basic innerness: the source of our subjective spontaneity, however minimal, concealed or profound. Its manifestation or birth can only be assisted and wished for – and certainly not determined or caused. It is an attitude that is hardly ever inappropriate, always sane, never expressed too soon or too late in any psychotherapeutic itinerary. When one thinks that it is too late to be spontaneous, the belief still functions as a regret for not having expressed one's spontaneity – a regret that indicates how precious we believe it is. *A Life of One's Own* ends with Milner's 'discovery' that the hidden areas of herself were not just to be understood, dealt with and, so to speak, conquered, but could be trusted and relied upon. In them she 'made contact with her own source of life'.[44]

Liberation from the rigidity of repetition and the creation of a new order for primitive currents cannot derive from theory, doctrine or education; it can only be attempted in the quasi-ineffable, serious inner experience of the individual who dares to be born. One cannot quite 'recover' from the experience of being born, cannot simply eliminate pain, but one can become curious about the future and even develop a sense of *amor fati*. But then, we should also ask why this venture may ultimately prove too difficult and virtually hopeless. A possible scenario suggested by Winnicott is that faulty environmental conditions may allow an external factor to impinge on the infant before he can manage it. This is a very basic notion in the sense that many of us live through so much that is unmanageable. Nevertheless, Winnicott focuses on a particular feature in the experience of the unmanageable, a moment in which the developing person is threatened with ego loss, with the danger of not being able to be born. 'What is uncanny about this loss is that the 'experience' involves a loss of the capacity to experience. . . . The capacity to sustain such a vicissitude has not yet developed.'[45] And yet, one of Winnicott's most striking remarks is that the madness that cannot be experienced is 'what is absolutely personal to the individual'.[46] We could also wonder whether this so-called madness is the truly personal part of the individual that hopefully seeks to be born, to gain access to the process of mentation, and that it is only mad because it stays where it is and is not properly born into the light of relational and symbolic life.[47]

In connection with Winnicott's remark to the effect that external factors may impinge on the developing self before it can manage the experience, we should also bear in mind that alongside an infant's need for relatedness there is, in fact, the need for a private space.[48] The infant can be 'fuelled' from without as well as from within. Modell reiterates that disengagement, as a desire to be born, has a place of equal importance with engagement.[49] If the private self becomes unfocused, one may lose contact with it, and one may also lose a sense of psychic aliveness and spontaneity. A private, uninvaded mental space is the condition for the birth of what we may call 'epistemophily' – a desire for thinking and knowing – as contrasted with 'epistemology' – a frame of mind deriving from cultural sources and to which one has to adapt.[50] There is thus a high price exacted when there is an occupation of the inner space by external paradigms, or when it is so firmly encapsulated that we have no contact with this innermost part of the self and cannot even hope for it to be born. These contingencies seem to function as the exact contrary of psychic midwifery. Modell reminds us that in some character pathologies there seems to be an unexplainable vindictive rage, as if the self had been totally usurped, or as if it were constantly besieged and excluded from the opportunities of life.[51] But, of course, psychopathology only illuminates by exaggeration that which occurs in all of us.

It is an essential passage in human development when creatures can not only get in touch with their feelings, but also move through steps of unfolding and growth. We can thus be moving beyond conformity patterns. The practice of maieutics replaces these patterns with the capacity to create new ones. Some people can get in touch with their feelings – but then what? They have 'visceral' feelings all right, but then the feelings do not ultimately change, perhaps not even in the encounter with mutative interpretations – as theorized by Strachey.[52] A further development is probably needed after getting in touch with feelings. A different kind of inward attention should be developed for what is at first sensed unclearly. When we nurture our feelings into a sufficient focus, then we may sense a psychic shift and if this does not happen, then perhaps there is no growth. Being born in this way can be a bewildering event, but the experience basically feels like a good one. Without psychic birth, one may perhaps attain a better self-understanding but with no change, and perhaps get in touch with feelings but not be able to let them move, shift, evolve into new forms of psychic life.

Much of our fear is apparently fear of change, of abandoning a status quo, a fear that we might lose whatever we have if we venture away from whatever is ruling the inner stage. But, in fact, we find new information distinctly threatening because if we incorporate it we will have to do a good deal of work to replace the protagonists of the show – the stars, the 'idols' – and we instinctively seek to avoid that work.[53] We can almost come to fight against illuminating insights rather than enhance their assimilation. The resistance is apparently motivated by 'fear', but then the instigator of fear is indolence, apathy, torpor – essentially passivity. It is actually fear of the work that one would have to do. It seems that sloth is a form of entropy as it manifests itself in our psychic lives. Why take the more active path, the option of more effort rather than less? Why take the path of breathing and eating instead of simply depending on some form of umbilical cord – or coerced transfusion? This is the persecutory, powerful pull of passivity or, conversely, the illusion of attaining knowledge just through eating the famous apple. Sloth is one of the less popular of the 'seven deadly sins', but whether or not it is a sin, it is psychically deadening.

In a reversed perspective of passivity, Nietzsche had already pointed out that the capacity to make a promise results in a 'memory of our will', in a conquest of the 'mental laziness of forgetting'.[54] Similarly, Ricoeur explores the nature of keeping a promise as the creative way of developing agentive selfhood.[55] In the psychoanalytic domain, Rosenfeld maintains that a sense of futility and passivity is more devastating than trauma, and he, conversely, elaborated at length on the intense pleasure of experiencing the good functioning of one's mind, or the 'immense joy' of being psychically alive.[56]

Psychodiversity and co-optosis

These neologisms are used to indicate the risk that our rich variety of psychic modes of survival – our psychodiversity – may be inconspicuously domesticated and absorbed into major homogeneous types, or even that indifference towards our inner development may induce an inclination to always seek admission to dominant systems – co-optosis. Aspiring to epistemic homogenization could be a mental narcotic that would damage psychodiversity if unexpected interrogation, or crises, did not occasionally expose its futility.[57]

We need not fear what might appear as chaos. Forthcoming is only a 'chaos' of plurality, plurivocity and differences that resist the reductivism of universality and univocity. Only to individuals constrained into a rigid conception of orthodoxy could this multiplicity be interpreted as chaotic in a derogatory sense. Not being sufficiently free for thinking and creativity can be a major crippling conflict, aggravated by a latent sense of guilt about refusing to homogenize with official sources of knowledge, or about resisting the seductions of some idealized 'pure reason'. When subjects recognize that this homogenization can be detrimental to contacts with one's own deep subjectivity, they may be freer to overcome some perverse sense of guilt about the effort to be a spontaneous and separate person, which would indeed be a sense of separateness that cannot, or should not, be resolved. In Scheman's view, we need to explore the appalling extent to which any person (culture, or part of the self) has been reduced to the 'dreams' and theories of any reigning coalition of 'theorists'; and yet, any marginalized person, or part of the self, can hold on to his deeply felt, though perhaps unaccountable, untheorizable conviction that he is something *other* than the product of those 'dreams' and theories.[58] In general, the subject who aspires to embody some dominant ideal most typically derives a definition of that ideal from imploded representations. The subject thereby surrenders all negotiating distance with respect to any ideality, as well as personal agency within the larger domain of interactions. He is not only compliant with whatever are the dominant values but is also deprived of any capacity to put values to new use, or to work transformatively upon them. This subject can only passionately – but passively – reaffirm the specular status quo.[59]

Indeed, developing 'a mind of one's own' is generally seen as a primary goal of the psychoanalytic experience.[60] It is commonly argued that the therapeutic process should aid analysands to utilize the complex vicissitudes of identification with early caretakers and analysts only in order to progressively identify with the result of their *own* experience and to create a privileged relationship with their own inner world. And this is not just a problem for the patient or for the therapist who tries to help: as a problem, it is clinically essential and culturally incumbent.

By refusing to be fixed in a fictional character emanating from passively internalized world views, we can perhaps also monitor the dangers of mimetic subjection to whoever appears as the emissary of an admirable, dominant epistemology. At times, individuals may even be inclined to mute their passion for their profound identity in order to create a spurious harmony with the theorizing that they most admire. The damaging attempt to be like-minded with the authorial authorities of culture almost requires breaking the passionate links that we have with our own inner world. Doing this, however, impedes proper contacts with one's constitutional self – and one's potential for spontaneity. We may thus sadly abandon our sources of affective growth in order to adhere to the constraining power (not 'force', but in fact just 'power') of whatever coalition of inner objects comes to appear as the 'enlightenment' of the moment.[61] This sort of contact with one's ideas and values also implies something of an exclusionary outlook: it establishes some sort of barrier between oneself and the external (or internalized) emissaries of whatever power insofar as one's own primary convictions inevitably differ from those of the 'authorities'.[62] From such figures one can derive more power than force, and power can be so overwhelming that we may lose contact with personal sources of force.

To be co-opted among the 'enlightened' is to be among the 'sane' and the 'winners'; for different creatures to join these ranks just requires a disposition to 'simply' *separate* from the difference-bearing aspects of our identity, our most intense particularity, such as curiosity for one's epistemophily and the lack of interest in any dominant epistemology. Thus, 'our' enlightened vocabulary also serves to demonstrate what any popular and democratic classicity seems to propagate: that one does not have to be a standard person in order to embrace elitist attitudes with regard to different others (or different parts of one's own self).[63]

The logic of any current classicity is an outlook that probably anyone can, or 'should', acquire by 'simply' insulating one's inner kernel of creativity. And the inclination to accept these enticements ultimately comes to appear as the soundest of attitudes. It is almost as if we could be deceived not only by falsity but also by truth, in the sense that any decontextualized truth can be misleading in an inconspicuous way. This is a nameless and denuding inclination that could perhaps be called 'co-optosis', in the sense that as long as one primarily aspires to be co-opted into the privileged ranks (inner or outer), one does ultimately sacrifice individual resources, or what could be called 'psychodiversity'.[64]

The resistance to abstractions, for the sake of enhancing the psycho-diversity of our inner 'others', can be fruitfully contrasted with the clau-strophilic and homogeneous language of inner idols. Conversely, the expressions of our epistemophily do not claim to be sources of authority, in the sense that they primarily insist – and insist they do, with precision, acumen and far-sightedness – that very different creatures exist and also have something to contribute. The tentative and inchoate language of our epistemophily is not geared to unassailable argumentation; its aims are in the direction of exploring diversity, complexity and spontaneity.

Even being a psychoanalyst is a particular way of being a person. There is no such thing as being a 'psychoanalyst', or a 'person', in the abstract.[65] There is only whatever unique analyst or person someone manages to be through one's unique process of coping with life. Psychoanalysis is both a profession *and* a way of being alive. It is the uniquely appropriate choice by which the analyst expresses who he is. And yet, the subjectivity and individuality of this way of being seems incongruent with the need for analysis to be grounded in general principles of theory and clinical tech-nique. In fact, paradox and compromise may be at work illuminating this contingency.

Bollas appropriately introduces a distinction between 'destiny' and 'fate' and posits an innate impulse to use others so as to enhance the potential of our true self.[66] This impulse sustains the expression of one's individual idiom, and to live according to that idiom is to make life a continuing act of self-discovery and self-creation. Creatures on this itinerary are working out a destiny for themselves. If one is preoccupied, instead, with a need of hom-ogenization, the sense is less of living one's life than of being at the mercy of fate. But then, we also feel that the seeker of destiny and the resistor to fate – the 'I' – is indeed vulnerable and in constant need of being protected. In fact, any form of initiative entails both risk and a willingness to act unilaterally whenever prompted by this destinal (destiny-oriented) part of the self. When our initiatives are not motivated in this way, they result as mere ploys and inevitably meet with counterploys.[67] In fact it may take people a lifetime to develop appropriate psychic 'filters' that work for them so as to facilitate the expression of the difference-bearing aspects of the seeker of destiny. And in connection with this, Eigen eloquently remarks that what we want and what our personality could bear do not always match.[68]

Envy and 'agency'

As an antithesis to spontaneity, envy could be seen as a form of pseudo-agency bordering upon malign passivity – that is, inclining towards attitudes of offence, resentment and impotence. The severity and regularity of this condition should elicit interest and attention rather than just plain dislike. The point is whether the 'active', inner vicissitudes of envy can help us explore the affliction of pseudoagency – both socially and individually. Kierkegaard offers an enlightening *aperçu* of this unfortunate condition: 'For what is offence? Offence is unhappy admiration. Thus it is related to envy, but it is an envy that turns against the person himself, is worse against oneself to an even higher degree. . . . The more passion and imagination a person has . . . the more passioned is his offence, which finally cannot be satisfied with anything less than getting this (the object of envy) rooted out, annihilated. . . . Envy is secret admiration. An admirer who feels that he cannot become happy by abandoning himself to it, chooses to be envious of that which he admires. . . . Admiration is happy self-surrender; envy is unhappy self-surrender.'[69] This is quite a sad contingency.

As a psychic attitude too unpleasant to admit to the world, great care is taken to camouflage it, usually also 'disguising' it from ourselves. Degrees of envy exist, of course. Epstein remarks that 'where envy turns ugly is when it turns pure: when . . . one does not even require any advantage for oneself but is perfectly content to make sure that the next person derives no advantage'.[70] The initial, inconspicuous stage of envy could perhaps be seen in 'idealization'. But then, if we refer to idealization, it has to mean that we actually *do* something in order to idealize, to perceive someone in an idealized way. What we do is perhaps to rid ourselves of our own good qualities and push them into the other person – indeed, without any gain or pleasure, apart from the hypothetic salvage of good things from our corrosive inner world. And Epstein asks why it is that some people feel envy just fleetingly, others use it towards emulation, and still others let it build to a poisoning level: 'Envy, by its very nature, is obstinate in its opposition to investigation and its protean character and talent for disguise probably account for the infrequency of studies on the subject.'[71]

The use of a psychoanalytic focus does not imply the generalized acceptance of strict Freudian models such as the idea of 'penis envy'; in fact, this is not to be interpreted as a woman's envy towards the masculine, but, rather, as the envy of both men and women who do not feel competent enough to fulfil desire in relation to those who are regarded competent: those who can act and not merely react, those who are not ensnared in the futility of envious reactions. Whatever else it is, envy is a great waste of mental energy, and, moreover, compared to the other six 'deadly sins', it gives no pleasure at all. Of course, we do waste precious energies detesting the envied, 'admired', competent others, but perhaps it is the *inner* state of envy that is actually hated and unbearable; it is this hatred that imprisons us. Symington points out that a quite frequent device to overcome the problem is the 'denial of what the person actually secretly envies. Things are turned around, and the person generates envy. In this type of situation the person . . . generates envy in those around, and then they can identify with the external envy, avoiding experiencing any of the hateful destruction of the self that goes on inside.'[72]

It is a question here of the massive projection of the inner state of envy into external others. In fact, if we could regard scriptures as indications of the psychology of a culture, the story of the Tower of Babel could be psychologically instructive: 'Come, let us build ourselves a tower with its top reaching heaven. Let us make a name for ourselves, so that we may not be scattered about the whole earth.'[73] Why be scattered about? If we can manage to be admired, we can become the object of the others' envy, and thus we can deal with the problem of envy externally – that is, in the others – which is much easier than coping with it inside ourselves. And, of course, if the tower could reach the heavens, our grandiose aspirations would be fulfilled with comparatively minor efforts. And also, why not have a name for oneself? If we have a name – a brand, a logo, a title or an established image – we need no longer worry about the personal source of our actions. Once one belongs to the right group, caste, company or fraternity, our wildest narcissism can be exercised without any personal sense of effort or remorse. Once you are a '___', you automatically become entitled to '___' – without any personal action, without being responsible for intentions.

From this same perspective, the entire domain of advertising could be viewed as little more than a bland, soft and acceptable envy-creating and envy-managing mechanism. Displaying all sorts of *de luxe* items, both tangible and symbolic, advertisements suggest that all of one's desires are ultimately within reach. They are not quite within reach of course, but even if they were, one's condition of envy would not be significantly trans-formed: further advertising of whatever kinds of 'goods' would insure against that.[74]

Especially with regard to the projection of envy onto the outside world, we could also note that the interest in celebrity ultimately feeds on people's curiosity. In this connection, Rose suggests that we might try to invert the expected formula – that celebrities are the people we are most curious about – and suppose instead that we require celebrities so as to let a very special form of envious curiosity off the leash: envy, from *in-videre*, 'looking into'. The intense curiosity feels dangerous for those who go in search of it as much as it does for those who are the target of it; it feels shameful in direct proportion to the frenzy with which it is pursued.[75] It could be a new edition of a very primitive level of relating that we commonly indicate as 'eating with the eyes', which is in fact an archaic way of interacting that is somehow rendered appealing and acceptable. 'Eating with the eyes' is perhaps a most furtive and secretive way of capturing something, and this is more easily managed when the role of the envier can be passed on to someone else.

From a Kleinian perspective, as is known, envy is about the pursuit by the child for the mother's breast – and the child wants no competitors.[76] In *Envy and Gratitude*, Klein also argues that the very envious creature is insatiable; he can never be satisfied because envy stems from within and therefore will always find an object to focus on. The child is even envious of the satisfactory breast. Although the infant feels gratified by it, the very ease with which the milk comes also gives rise to envy because this capacity for donating gifts seems unattainable. But, of course, these vicissitudes remain largely unconscious. And so one can envy just about everything, even those things one knows that one should not have. One can envy the extravagant dangerous possession, or the job that would ultimately aggravate life. 'But then, whoever said that envy makes sense?' – remarks Epstein.[77] In a lucid, synoptic *aperçu*, Symington suggests that these illusory perceptions are the result of unconscious dynamics: 'To speak with psychological accuracy, we need to say that the perception records correctly what has emotionally occurred.'[78] Conversely, if we shift our point of observation from a psychoanalytic perspective onto a historical view, we could say that Marxism also strenuously attempted to provide a persuasive argument for the origin of envy. The heroic revolution of the proletariat that it propagated was perhaps a promise to eliminate the social conditions that make for envy. Marxism perhaps even posited human nature as yearning for equality as the basis for what cogency it might possess. Perhaps the class struggle is about nothing less than the enviable advantages that the upper classes have over the lower – advantages that even at the cost of hurtful revolutions must be eliminated. But then, the expulsion of inner vicissitudes onto the socio-historical stage does not prove so illuminating after all.

Resentment could be regarded as a 'variant' of envy which also determines futile forms of pseudoagency propelled by bitter criticism, spite and detraction. Envy and resentment (with its constant sense of injustice) are not always easily distinguished, let alone extricated one from the other. The similarities and distinctions between those two states of mind cannot perhaps be made entirely clear. By way of example, Epstein remarks that academics often feel themselves greatly superior and vastly undervalued with respect to other creatures, insufficiently rewarded and revered: 'They have about them a perpetually disappointed air; one senses that they feel that the world has, somehow, let them down.'[79] Those who suffer from resentment do not believe that much of anything can be done to remedy the source of their resentful attitude. Epstein quotes Scheler as suggesting that resentment can only arise if its emotions are particularly powerful, and yet, 'they must be suppressed because they are coupled with the feeling that one is unable to act them out – either because of weakness . . . or because of fear.'[80] And, of course, this ends in an acceptable, sophisticated way of embittering the personality. The 'actions' to be enjoyed are the occasions for criticism that the outlook allows. And yet the criticisms propelled by resentment do not imply or even advocate the eradication of what is considered wrong, because in this case 'the growing pleasure offered by invective and negation'[81] would be entirely lost. In fact, in a psychic atmosphere of resentment, not even pseudoaction seems plausible, for it is the element of impotence that seems to make for resentment. The secret vicissitudes of envy seem to only end in resentment when we come to believe that we can do nothing about them.

A cultural perspective

Even the most elitist and most enlightened of creatures can be the victims of psychic passivity – this most damaging affliction. The temptation to succumb to a particular phantasmal power is so intense that most of us are vulnerable to it. It could be instructive to ponder over the case of the celebrated writer, Virginia Woolf. Without any claim to subscribe to the historical accuracy of the anecdote, it is interesting to note that Woolf is reported as having passively succumbed to the obscure fascination of national socialism. Rose actually refers to her as a fiercest critic of dictators, as one who never 'came anywhere near to slipping into . . . fascist identification'.[82] And yet, Rose goes on to write that perhaps one of the 'strangest' things she did was to travel to Germany on holiday when the belligerent vigour of anti-Semitism was clear, and to record in her diary, 'There is some reason I suppose to expect that Oxford Street will be flooded with poison gas these days.'[83] In the course of this same trip, when 'suddenly caught in the middle of a flag-waving crowd of Nazi supporters shouting *Heil Hitler*, she raised her arm in salute'.[84] And once again, the damaging affliction of passivity seems to strike her; we read in Rose: 'Five years later, caught in an air raid . . . she stood still and lifted her arms to the sky.'[85]

The author judiciously remarks that if there is something idolatrous about her salute, 'there is something no less puzzling and scary about her wartime embracing of the night sky. What might lead someone, in a state of real potential danger, to identify with, stretch out towards – yearn for – the aggressor? What might lead someone to seem passionately to covet what they most fear?'[86] Whatever truth there is in the report, it can certainly serve as an indication of the insidious and perverse nature of psychic passivity. The sort of passivity that can infect anyone.

If any true revolution is one of our inner self, it requires not only the creation of positive values for those abjected by dominant culture, but also the revaluation of values such that the very structure of valuation is opened up for transformation. It requires throwing off not only Marxism's imaginary chains, but also the chains that bind our imagination and thereby asphyxiate the self. In Oliver's view, 'This new valuation must begin from the subjected position of those othered. They – we – must articulate the meaning of our own lives and thereby transform the very means of production of value. . . . Moreover decolonization of psychic space begins with understanding the dynamics of the colonization of psychic space and how it invades body and soul . . . soul and body.'[87] As an isolated being – insists Fromm – the individual is helpless in comparison to the potentially colonizing outside world and therefore deeply afraid. 'He is therefore overcome by doubts concerning himself. . . . Both helplessness and doubt paralyse life and in order to live man tries to escape from freedom, negative freedom. He is driven into new bondage. . . . The escape does not restore . . . security but only helps him to forget his self as a separate entity. He finds new and fragile security at the expense of sacrificing the integrity of his individual self. He chooses to lose his self since he cannot bear to be alone. Thus freedom – as freedom-from – leads into new bondage.'[88] And of course, freedom-from is quite different with respect to freedom-to, which is a capacity for initiative, intentionality and creativity.

The question is why those othered and abjected within a relationship (or within a culture) ultimately internalize the very 'values' that abject and oppress them, as we have seen in a glimpse of Woolf's vicissitudes. And yet, attaining a psychic unicity does not mean the end of conflict but, rather, a flexible and resilient integration of one's own type of psychological maturity. In fact, the idealization of an abjecting culture cannot just simply be eliminated. Silverman claims that we cannot argue against idealization – without which human existence would be unendurable, and which is the precondition for every access to the other, whether identificatory or erotic – but against the *smooth* meshing of that psychic operation with culturally defined norms.[89] The colonization of our processes of idealization emanating from the success of mainstream culture not only restricts ideality to certain objects, smoothly 'naturalized' as essentially ideal, but also renders other objects unworthy of admiration. We thus need to learn how to idealize oppositionally and provisionally. A variant of this formulation is that some empathic subjects turn into less sophisticated readers of the cultural images that define them; they somehow tip over into the mirror of cultural representation and come to imagine – erroneously – that they really are what it defines them as being.[90]

As a category, the agents of mainstream epistemology and colonization have no canonical or fixed historical content. But then, they are *persons* who think, and they are embodied and situated in specific contexts. And their culturally situated embodiment is somehow relevant to their actual modes of thinking and feeling.[91] In their situatedness, thinking beings are significantly different from the abstract, 'pure', context-independent perennial ideals with which we should homogenize. The potentially epistemophilic individuals also differ from these ideals in that they not only shape but also undergo and absorb experience, and thus steadily contribute to their own psychodiversity. One of the merits of feminist epistemology is the recognition that 'pure' epistemology is no longer possible: it is a fracture from a tradition that does not acknowledge the specificity of its sources. The autonomy obsession of logocentric thinking endorses a stark conception of individualism that overemphasizes self-realization and self-reliance; feminists frequently argue against the supremacy of these values in favour of 'second personhood' and mutuality. But the psychoanalytic point is that it would be a mistake to conflate individualism and psychodiversity, so that when criticizing narcissistic individualism we might also ignore or even repudiate our precious individuality.[92]

Our human community is marked by many more differences than are contained in our 'philosophies', differences that proliferate as we try to define them. But how, then, do we characterize differences and individuality? The question is whether they are conceived as natural facts that the person passively reflects, or else whether they can be regarded as features that can be willed and hence made active aspects of the subject's relation to a sense of self. We are commonly the inheritors or followers of other people's styles, but we also have the opportunity to locate subjective agency in the specific internal connections that we weave out of that heritage.

In our contemporary world the individual is increasingly caught in a global net in the sense that the flow of information and resources simultaneously involves us with the whole planet, thus turning the individual into a citizen of the 'global village'. On the other hand, the person is more and more drawn into the search for real or even imaginary cultural roots in what seems to be a desperate – or even cruel – search for individual identity. The fragmentation of this global ideal may be seen as a compensation for belonging to a world increasingly shaped by large-scale forces that are well beyond the control of individuals; and we thus have an ongoing tension between individuation and globalization.

Consider, for instance, the affiliates of a gang chief, the reports of a corrupt corporate boss, or a group of ideologized extremists enacting the will of their leaders. It appears that, in their case, perverse principles can still give rise to the good qualities of daring and courage. But perhaps things are not as simple as they might superficially appear. When a powerful collective pull substitutes for our personal spontaneity and confers a homogenized collective identity, adherents are more afraid of the merciless wrath of the aggregating perversion than they are of the actual dangers that threaten their own lives. As a result, they place themselves in the position of risking their physical lives for the sake of protecting their psychic life – however imitative or perverse. Passivity may thus reveal itself as a form of illness, or necessity.

Chapter 5

The problem of entitlement

Freud's 'Exceptions'

Analysts frequently encounter subjects who bear the consequences of trauma and who also feel entitled to a variety of compensations. The thesis is that there should be special attention and empathy for the ongoing condition of being caught in the psychic attitude of demanding compensation, just as there is awareness and empathy for their previous imprisonment in conditions of neglect and abuse.

Being entitled to any narcissistic behaviour on account of previous suffering can be seen as an encompassing pathology that is both quite common and vulnerable to obscurity. Having been confined to situations of neglect and/or abuse, individuals may become restrained in an outlook of entitlement of their own making; which is the contrary of spontaneity. In 'Some Character-Types Met With in Psychoanalytic Work', Freud remarks in the section 'The Exceptions' that whenever analysts invite patients to make a provisional renunciation for the sake of a better prospect or 'to submit to a necessity which applies to everyone, one comes upon individuals who resist such an appeal on a special ground. They say that they have renounced enough and suffered enough, and have a claim to be spared any further demands; they will submit no longer to any disagreeable necessity, for they are *exceptions* and, moreover, intend to remain so.'[1] And he continues that, of course, 'Their neuroses were connected with some experience of suffering to which they had been subjected in their earliest childhood, one in respect to which they knew themselves to be guiltless and which they could look upon as an unjust disadvantage imposed upon them.'[2] And thus the privileges that they claim in order to compensate for this injustice, and the resentment that it engenders, may concur in the pathology of these subjects. The 'exceptions' in fact do not feel guilty because they consider their entitlement justified through prior pain.

Freud insists that everyone, to a degree, thinks of himself as an exception with special claims and demands, even though not everyone believes himself to be an exception to all rules. In Freud's view, the 'exceptions' are those who have seriously suffered and thus have *already* 'paid the price' for any occasion of pleasure. The term 'exception' seems to imply a statistical dimension, indicating a deviance from the norm in the sense that an exception is a rarity. But the problem is that, to varying degrees of severity, most of us may secretly believe that we truly *are* exceptions. But then, as McDougall reiterates, we all are 'psychic survivors'.[3] In fact, pathology only amplifies an attitude that we all share to some degree – namely, the more or less profound conviction that on account of previous difficulties we are entitled to obtain, or extort, whatever we believe we 'deserve'.

With reference to Shakespeare's *Richard III*, Freud remarks that he 'is an enormous magnification of something we find in ourselves as well. . . . We all demand reparation for early wounds to our narcissism.'[4] In the strenuous effort to compensate for the cumulative experiences of deprivation, the individual is not hindered by ambivalences of any kind; the whole inner 'script' may then become a rigid and repetitive pattern. And failures, of course, only strengthen the perverse explanatory theory, as if we were saying, 'Once again I am being cheated of what I need so badly, and I must therefore try even harder.' This lifestyle may result in the caricature of a vocation in that it lacks any spontaneity and is only propelled by constriction. In the event of being offered attention and compassion while not being able to get to the root of one's distress, the individual feels that whatever is received is somehow defective and always insufficient.

The crucial question is why others did have caring parents – and not the suffering person – and why there is a continuation of these vicissitudes. Once the injustice of the other person having had loving care is established – and this can be easily accomplished – the 'therapeutic' strategy becomes totally clear. Human coexistence seems to be absurd as long as others have had the cares we haven't. The quality of one's feelings in connection with this matter may become obsessional – at the opposite end of spontaneity. Our basic concepts, moreover, are interwoven so closely with what is most fundamental to our way of living that they become unassailable. If one is clever and retains some self-control, he will know not to speak about anything to do with the theme. If one is less clever and haemorrhagic, he will too often talk about it, and even reveal his plans for redressing the harm. There should, perhaps, be a better awareness of this ongoing problem, and also empathy for this painful condition.

Freud points to Richard III as a figure in whose character the claim to be an exception is also motivated by conditions of congenital disadvantage.[5] Richard's physical deformity could be a metaphor for his deformed character, as well as its cause. Freud refers to the congenital defects of Shakespeare's character as of someone thrown into the world inside a crippled and malformed body, so lame and unfashionable that dogs bark at him; Richard says: 'As I cannot play the lover on account of my deformity, I will play the villain; I will intrigue, murder, and do anything else I please.'[6] He *can* intrigue and murder: having paid his dues in prior suffering he can now freely inflict suffering with self-righteous pride. He perhaps exemplifies the more primitive narcissistic, sadistic personality in which self-love is alloyed with hatred and self-hate. Freud insists that having renounced and suffered enough while feeling unfairly treated, those who believe that they are exceptions will no longer submit to any disagreeable necessity 'and moreover intend to remain so'. Clinging to a privileged position becomes a formidable style of psychic life as well as a resistance to the development of spontaneity. And Freud instructively paraphrases the words of Richard III: 'Nature has done me grievous wrong in denying me the beauty of form which wins human love. Life owes me reparation for this, and I will see that I get it. I have a right to be an exception, to disregard the scruples by which others let themselves be held back. I may do wrong myself, since wrong has been done to me.'[7]

Richard III ultimately says that it is on account of his sufferings that he feels entitled to 'intrigue, murder and do anything else he pleases'. 'Such a frivolous motivation' – writes Freud – 'could not but stifle any stirring of "sympathy" in the audience, if it were not a screen for something much more serious . . . and such sympathy can only be based . . . on a sense of a possible inner fellow-feeling for him.'[8] In fact, the vast diffusion of psychoanalytic literature, together with the more popular versions of it, can often be used to accurately appreciate the adverse developmental effects of traumatic vicissitudes – which perhaps many of us have suffered. As a consequence we become enabled to construct some 'scientifically' based model of special entitlement in our minds.

A damaging affliction

In Weil's view, 'That which is the direct opposite of an evil never belongs to the order of a higher good. It is often scarcely any higher than evil.'[9] Entitlement could perhaps be explored from this perspective. In the attitude of entitlement we seem to say, 'Pleasure is the good we need: the exact contrary of the frustrations we endured. The situation must be reversed at all costs.' One feature of this damaging condition is the view of oneself having been forced into a hopeless psychic state *together* with the demand for total healing; this is to be achieved by means of the magnificent and 'evidential' virtues of a correctly practised psychoanalytic treatment. Such a submissive, idealizing and coercive request of a sure result seems to closely approximate a demand for drug treatment. The result being 'certain', one may immediately start thinking of what will happen after analysis – and resign from inner work. Although most of us are tempted to do 'anything that we please', through the aid of interrogating psychoanalytic theories we can transform this simple temptation into a legitimate right. And, of course, those who are legitimately, 'scientifically' entitled to compensation may ultimately 'succeed' in their pursuits more easily than those who are merely tempted.

But then, the question is how one can be spontaneous when crushed by historical circumstances or afflicted by serious mental illness. The point is that in extreme psychic or interpersonal conditions, we may be inclined to ignore any resources of creativity, libido, cognition, imagination that we may have. This unfortunate propensity may be negatively influenced by the use of innumerable psychological 'doctrines' in the sense that adverse conditions are utilized to *causally explain* the inexorable destruction of any personal agency; once this destruction is 'scientifically' accounted for, one may surreptitiously feel entitled to a total surrender while also tranquilly entitled to exert all means in order to exact compensations.[10]

In commenting on Kohut's view of empathic self-objects, Symington argues that he allows no place for inner resources and concludes: 'The predicate is that a person's psychopathology is due to unattuned selfobjects, so all the bad is out there and we have a theory with a paranoid base.'[11] But then, a theory with a 'paranoid base' would only allow for reactions and manipulations, along with the foreclosure of actions proper, for our potential of forgiveness – indeed, our genius of forgiveness. Symington's view is that such theories do instigate the development of paranoia and the asphyxiation of creativity. From this same perspective, Blum suggests that 'compensation is a means to redress injury, to obtain justice and a reparation for pain and loss'.[12] As is known, the need for compensation takes many forms, including the conviction of being entitled to extra love, comfort and sympathy from others – in an insatiable manner. Conversely, a more mature sense of agency might enable us to enjoy 'small' things; when we passively seek total compensation, we can be desperate in spite of being satisfied to an exceptional high degree. 'Small' joys thus become difficult to detect and appreciate.

Entitlement may be associated with the projection of guilt and blame onto others, or with the reaction formation of excessive humility and modesty. Blum remarks that an individual may not be aware of regarding himself as an exception and consequently as an unacknowledged privileged character.[13] The lack of conscious shame or guilt may be associated with self-righteous and self-justified attitudes. Those who are above rules often make their rules and try to impose them on others. One of the most striking characteristics that Freud noted is the apparent absence of guilt and the absolute conviction of privilege, tinged with infantile omnipotence. Blum insists that patients who are 'exceptions' often have a sense of righteous indignation and are determined to show the analyst the correct notions of right and wrong. They have been wronged and are right to belittle, criticize and condemn others for their real or hypothetic faults. In feeling justified because they have been wrongly mistreated, they attempt to extract apologies or even confessions from the analyst, parent or others who have damaged them. Their own sense of inadequacy can be managed by focusing on the defects of others; experts in fault-finding, they avoid or minimize self-criticism. 'Complaints of abuse and deprivation are used to justify and rationalise their own aggression, hate and exploitation of others.'[14]

The problem is that in degree they may have been actually abused and neglected, and thus the escape from the psychic trap of entitlement needs to be most carefully planned. If the problem of entitlement is not sufficiently focused upon, even the most correct or prolonged therapeutic efforts may be defeated through the unconscious collusion of analysand and analyst. If the problem is sufficiently clarified, moreover, one may work at it while carefully avoiding any judgemental or infantilizing approach. In fact, any such approach may ultimately prevent maturational work in the sense that it will come across as an adversarial, unempathic response. This is especially so because, in the language of Blum, 'The exception has made a virtue out of adversity, and through projection and reversal, wrong becomes right meriting reward rather than punishment. The privileged position defends against further narcissistic injuries and traumata. . . . Incited with narcissistic rage when the satisfaction . . . is thwarted, they may be shameless and remorseless about infantile temper tantrums which may ensue.'[15] These individuals also tend to be quite ethical in some respects, while ruthless in other contingencies of life. 'Megalomaniac invincibility may coexist in some exceptions with extreme vulnerability to narcissistic mortification. These exceptions, like Richard III, may be driven to attain power and position, to re-invent themselves in a glorified rather than defective form.'[16] These characters present a compromise formation whereby they feel undeserving *and* entitled, self-punitive *and* omnipotently privileged. As Freud clearly emphasized, there is something of the exception in all of us, a bid for privileged position and special entitlement.

The conviction of being entitled to restitution does not easily sustain elaboration, for the belief is far more appealing than any other view; it is a trick that *must* function, and it must work because psychic offence was in fact suffered – and thus repayment due. The trick *is* the treat in the logic of entitlement. Totally obvious, the conviction seems impossible to eradicate; vulnerable to obscurity, the conviction is not only unassailable, but it entitles the creature to the use of any strategy. There is indeed no limit to what one should attempt for the sake of a righteous and obvious concern. Paradoxically, as everything is due to one, no effort is required and thus one may become definitely passive; but one may also become tranquilly omnipotent because virtually everything is permitted for the sake of such a worthy goal. This damaging affliction is perhaps one of the chief usurpers of our potential for spontaneity.

Clinical implications

If self-righteousness is a form of dissociation implying that there is nothing wrong with one's own self, it must be difficult to treat subjects who survive by means of this psychic split; in the self-righteous individual, moreover, there seems to be an ongoing pleasure that is even drawn from emotionally destructive and sadistic currents. Through this attitude, personal attempts to relate to others seem doomed to fail. Accepting otherness is, in fact, a form of creativity that deviates from the pleasure of addressing the 'other' as an antagonist, as the bearer of error and evil. The 'preciousness' of self-righteousness can also be purchased from the adherence to appropriate groups, and thus becoming entitled to a powerful form of both dissociation and support. Pizer eloquently says that 'Group identity serves the individual group members' self-definition and integrity – . . . the illusion of self-simplification – by deployment of primitive mechanisms that provide for its subscribers a psychic excretion of perturbing, contradictory, threatening, burdensome, and otherwise challenging personal qualities.'[17] Underneath a veneer of compliance and false self, there seems to be a layer of rage in the form of craving for control and power; when more visible than it should be, this desire is justified as an attempt to finally abandon submissive compliance and is perhaps even mistaken for the quest for a true self.

In a psychic atmosphere of entitlement, relationships tend to become critical, for the other is insistently drawn into one's narcissistic outlook. A relationship implies two or more parties. If any two elements become homogenized into the same, there can no longer be a relationship between them. Intolerant of the relational, one of the ways in which vindictive entitlement operates is the attempt to destroy separateness.[18] There is thus a failure of separateness between 'the exceptions' and their others; they will assume that you think in the same way that they think. If you do not, they will be entitled to 'correct' and 'retrain' you – perhaps even out of 'love'.

The attitude of entitlement is often expressed in a language that is coercive, for arguments are best when they compel others into a conclusion – and are not so good when less cogent. There is a constant attempt to get someone to believe something whether he wants to share the belief or not. The successful argument coerces others into a belief. The ideal discourse would be the one that leaves no possible answers to the interlocutor, reducing him to impotent silence. In the language of Nozick, we 'need arguments so powerful that they set up reverberations in the brain: if the person refuses to accept the conclusion, he *dies*. How is that for a powerful argument? A "perfect" argument would leave no choice.'[19] But then Symington suggests that below the level of consciousness the person may actually feel bad about manipulating others, even though the coercive argument is quite subtle and accurately concealed with a display of generosity.[20] A common form of manipulation is to persuade people to give us psychic energy and motivation. And yet if we are not able to be the source of our own motivation, we may ultimately forswear our quest for spontaneity. The source of action in the healthy person is from within. The source of action in the agent of entitlement is at the surface, where one incorporates those contracted to provide motivation.[21] This route, however, is often conducive to failure, and thus, from this same logic, we seek to secure ever *better* external sources of support and more coercive means for recruiting them.

According to Symington, the self can be erotized through stimulating one's surface by oneself or by getting others to do so; but even if the subject does it himself, he has to conjure up a fantasy of another who performs for him; it is like an auto-erotic activity that has to be constantly elicited and renewed – even in a psychoanalytic context. In his view, there is a sense of shame when the analysand manages to attach himself to the place of the analyst's deficit, and this is the reason why it is crucial that the analyst's own deficits become elucidated. 'It's like a tree fungus that attaches itself to that part of the tree where the sap is coming out.'[22] It may turn into a saprophytic relation in which attempts at interpretation become futile while they allow for an inexplicable sense of guilt about attaching to the points of vulnerability. Of course, it is true that people who have suffered trauma are prone to adhesive and intrusive relations, but we could see this condition from a different perspective: these relations are not only the result of trauma but they become ongoing sources of psychic pain. The persons who are attracted into these relations are projected into, and so they experience the devastation of the suffering person. 'Entering' others and possessing them from within is one of the most primitive reactions to one's inner distress; in essence, intruding and possessing appear as the necessary precondition that allows for extorting compensation. When restitution is wanted at all costs, projecting and dominating appear as a necessary strategy. Inhabiting and controlling in order to obtain the love that one has not received probably results in failure, as it repeats the attitude of one's originary inadequate caretakers. It is a vicious circle that must be avoided through a constant concern for both thinking and patience. In fact, these invisibly suffering people cannot afford to work to develop their own spontaneity. To the extent that we see more clearly the fixity of their predicament and their scarce spontaneity, we can truly appreciate their obscure condition of suffering. When they try to violently intrude, they only provide an example of the seriousness of their affliction. There is in fact something that seems, at first sight, to be a contradiction. In the person who is most passive, there is at the same time the most virulent projective attitude. It is very common for someone who is definitely passive to be surrounded by people who are exasperated with such behaviour; the frustration is a sign that there are unbearable projections in the process.[23] In fact, the exasperation around those 'passive' subjects is actually generated by intense emotional exertion. Freud says that 'It is a very remarkable thing that the unconscious of one human being can react upon that of another, without passing through consciousness. This deserves closer investigation; . . . but, descriptively speaking, the fact is incontestable.'[24] And so the passivity of those who feel entitled to compensation of torts seems commonly accompanied by affective endeavours of high intensity. According to Symington, if what someone is saying is systematically not coming from initiatory action but almost entirely from a passive state geared towards getting others to act, then it is of no value responding to it. A patient may spend time mournfully recounting the neglect and abuse he has suffered for the purpose of controlling others.[25] But then, the analyst who takes the line that he is just going to be a neutral receptacle leaves the patient alone in his deadening condition.

There is a further aspect to the question of entitlement, namely the expression of hatred. In extreme synthesis, the story goes like this: the individual hates others because he has once been the object of hatred. In fact, the destructiveness of entitlement is not sustained by fleeting emotions but, rather, by a profound and diffuse sense of hatred. And here we face a typical case of arguments based on the idea of infinite regress or vicious circles. In this outlook, hatred presupposes hatred; there seems to be no real hatred that is not a reaction to having been hated. This position implies a peculiar deduction, namely that we cannot be the first ones to express hatred. But then, where does the chain begin? We could say that the question is not relevant for the clinician; but perhaps it is.[26] We do not quite know. What is essential is an initiatory capacity to try to 'break the chain', starting whenever the insertion of an alternative attitude is acceptable. In fact, the momentous step towards seeking help always brings with it a measure of knowledge, which is why it is so frequently avoided.[27] The grandiose side of the self always insinuates at such a moment that whatever one attempts is absolutely futile and that the vicious/'virtuous' circle of entitlement must go on. When the analyst is confronted with these situations, it is important to be aware of how delicate and insidious they can be. It is necessary to appreciate the internal dialectics of the subject and to express it in such a way that it can become visible and perspicuous. It is inappropriate to try to make the subject experience hope or gratitude instead, as it could be of no help. In Symington's view, 'The thing to do is to hold up the negativistic, self-pitying, vengeful mentality clearly to view, avoiding any flavour of condemnation.'[28] If the clinical thinking is sufficiently clear, no judgemental remarks would come forth.

The question of pseudoagency

The question of pseudoagency relates to ways of exerting psychic influence – which is not creative action but, rather, the result of futile attempts to surmount passivity. There is a constant need to try to focus on this question so as also to improve the insight into one's way of being an analyst; it is a matter of explicating the implicit principles that could be at work in pseudoagency and even in the therapeutic process. Whenever it is a question of compensations or of redressing torts, human action can easily deteriorate into pseudoaction – to the detriment of our potential for spontaneity. This attitude, moreover, may even determine our paradigms of behaviour, or in fact our principles. Just as unformulated or implicit experience generates the construction of principles, so too do the principles, once formulated, shape one's way of perceiving what we do. There is little sense, for the most part, in trying to determine which comes first. In both directions, moreover, the link is not simply an issue of cause and effect. There is some virtual 'space' between the source of influence and its impact, a gap in which we can be present as potential agents or discerning subjects. One may come to believe in strict causality in order to be entitled to exert control, incorporation and extortion; one may become entitled to this behaviour on account of all the frustrations endured and must consequently theorize such causality in order to envisage an unassailable policy of entitlement, which in turn determines a style of pseudoactions, however cunning and futile.

This problem seems to intensely resonate with our contemporary culture in the sense that it is frequently expressed in the myths of our most popular literature, as for instance the acclaimed *Harry Potter* saga. He Who Must Not Be Named has had a suicidal sort of mother and a deserting father, while *our* Harry Potter has had a heroic mother who would freely give her life to save her child – totally unsure of whether or not her sacrifice would be effective. His father would qualify as a 'good-enough' parent by Winnicottian standards. But then, this looks like an unfair share in parental love. Notwithstanding the hateful foster-parents, Harry turns into a sure winner, forever fooling and escaping You Know Who, the obsessive, 'passionate' destroyer of just about anything. The critical discriminant is Harry's inner energy, probably due to the sort of love – however quantitatively minimal – that makes us flourish. For, in fact, who cares about vindictive power if one has inner courage and sufficient self-esteem? Most of our myths are built around figures who have nothing but courage and a healthy respect for themselves. But what about those who do not: the creeps, the cowards, the vindictive envious, the rigidified victims of entitlement and the imitators – even re-styling themselves as 'ladies' and 'lords'? A homogenization of these features can possibly make for an astute killer who craves immortality and who ultimately destroys himself. It is indeed a fertile topic for reflection.

If the function of personal response comes to be theoretically excluded, the person becomes restricted into a very tight mechanism of cause and effect, which renders one prone to the highest degree of perverse entitlement.

If one is 'ontologically' entitled to having had caring parents and this has not been the case, then one seems to have the right to a non-negotiable compensation in terms of subsequent interpersonal strategies. If the compensation is not coming forth, it is actually a perverse 'ethical' duty to exert one's very best efforts in this concern, to exercise all of one's considerable ingenuity – horcruxes and all that. The individual *feels* that he should leave no depth of cunning unplumbed in this quest for compensating for whatever he has been deprived of. The best way to make sure that one is given love is to coerce the other to give as much love as is needed; to this effect, one should control the other by inhabiting the person and attuning the other's mind to one's own. This is done by inducing in the other a mental benumbment that facilitates control – that is, making him feed on one's epistemology, turn him into an 'eater' of a perverse logic, no less than that. Another strategy is to 'love' the other immensely so that he will at least feel guilty for not reciprocating such enormous affect and thus become amenable to submission. Epstein reports Farber as suggesting that whereas true admiration keeps the distance between the admirer and the admired, the assault by the righteous claim upon its object may take the form of envious flattery that serves not only its need to assert itself in the guise of admiration, but also the desire to capture the very quality that initially incited envy. The moral of the story is to 'watch the eyes of those who bow lowest'.[29] This attitude, moreover, presents pathology benefits in the sense that those who are firmly convinced that they deserve what they want are usually more 'successful' in obtaining just what they crave for. In some way they become virtuosi in the insatiable extortion of what they seek. In this ultimately pseudoagentive context, ordinary admiration turns into the pathology of envy.

This sort of pseudoagentive attitude seems to apply in particular to the very active, energetic, successful individuals who unconsciously strive to control and possess, no matter how adamantly they deny it. And yet, no matter how much we would like to be, we are not in charge of the whole situation. Once we accept that we are not in charge, we can let go of many preoccupations, and just try to live. It is probably a 'sufficient' degree of spontaneous agency that enables us to let go of things that are not our responsibility. In fact, our inadequate agency and our passivity may narcissistically ensnare us into believing that we are indeed in charge of the whole complex of events and thus determine a pseudoactive sense of futile activity. Through the quest for authentic agency we could discern what it is that counts for us – and do more of it. This 'noble' game of trying to control everything, while openly denying it, can develop into a falsifying attitude, and contemporary philosophy frequently resonates with this critical issue. In the words of Buber, this is 'the uncanny game of hide and seek in the obscurity of the soul, in which it, the single human soul, evades itself, hides from itself'.[30] In still another philosophical idiom, Wittgenstein argues that 'Lying to oneself about oneself, deceiving yourself about the pretence in your own state of will, must have a harmful influence on [one's] style; for the result will be that you cannot tell what is genuine in the style and what is false. . . . If I perform to myself, then it is this that the style expresses and then the style cannot be my own.'[31] By becoming impersonal we asphyxiate subjective agency.

This interlocked problem of denial and control is probably sustained by narcissistic currents in the personality. Grotstein offers a synopsis by suggesting that 'the narcissist uses the object, not in a normal sharing relationship for normal dependency and interdependency, but for a manipulative, parasitic relationship in which the object is to be seduced and controlled so as to allow the autistic/narcissistic subject to remain omnipotent and protectively encapsulated. . . . [T]he narcissist hates object relations but is stuck with them and so has to manipulate them to their pathological needs.'[32] Patients are in fact often of two minds; they may enter treatment out of both a desire to conquer *and* a desire to be healed. But sometimes the desire of conquest seems the prevalent one. And yet the patient might allow himself to be 'conquered' – that is, lose the battles he provokes – in order to win his soul. The insistence on controlling every aspect of the analytic relation is, in fact, rooted in fear: the dread that he may lose control of everything. Patients might even be secretly content with their impotence and omnipotence. Coming for help could even be a sad lie. An analyst who often feels confused, who cannot work with a sufficient feeling of clarity, may attribute his difficulties to his own inadequacy. And yet, perhaps, he may be confused because the patient's inner saboteur intends to confuse him; the patient may come for help with the decision of defeating any help. What gradually transpires is a desire to seduce, control and drain. And then one may wonder why a patient can stay in treatment as long as he does; it could be that the analyst offers him the ongoing pleasure of 'playing' with someone, together with the ongoing hope that he can succeed in conquering the therapist and his love. These analysands may remain somewhat enigmatic and the analyst confused – which is the way they might want it to be. They may withhold information if for no other reason than to keep control of the show. While the understanding of the patient is deepening, so is the analyst's awe of his basic incomprehensibility. They may fear that they cannot win the unconditional love of the analyst but also believe that with the wonderful gestures they do for him, he will eventually change his mind. But then, a patient cannot both possess his analyst and at the same time be an analysand. Perhaps they do not want to relinquish any power for any reason. They want healing but are not willing to give up anything in the process; they want to be nurtured while also being the tyrants of the nurturers. In the meanwhile, in their perception of themselves they are a great source of love and gentleness. Most of what the analyst and the others experience of him, however, can be the sense of chaos and confusion that they tend to leave in their wake, while constantly pretending that they just love others and want to be well.[33] When the propelling force of psychic behaviour is the conviction of being entitled to compensation and control, they ultimately act from a source that is discordant with respect to any potential for spontaneity. Those acting from a discordant source – reiterates Symington – benefit in that they can sail on in ignorance of this source: 'They do not have to know the nature of the traitor they harbour within. . . . The processes of their mind are always being interfered with and being cut off from the source of action, and so they are always victim.'[34] It is indeed an ongoing condition of pseudoagency.

The pathology of 'success'

To invoke still another philosophical outlook, we could refer to Kierkegaard's insight into the psychology of 'success'; with exemplary clarity he seems to point out that the problematic condition of pseudoagency – that is, the sort of agency that is not creative but only reactive – is ultimately unbearable. In Kierkegaard's view, in fact, despair is *The Sickness unto Death*,[35] an inner state for which success is no remedy at all. To put the question of pseudoagency in its extreme form, we could say that to be maximally agentive one ought to become powerful and famous – or, more precisely, *the* most powerful and *the* most famous. If we take Julius Caesar as a classical emblem of fame and authority, we can better understand the craving expressed in the saying 'Either Caesar or nothing' – that is, nothing short of being Caesar is acceptable. As is known, this was the motto of Caesar Borgia – the Duke Valentine – as presented in Machiavelli's *Prince*. But one does not have to be the handsome and gifted Borgia, as possibly anyone could secretly consider this aspiration. But then, in order to become 'Caesar', and nothing short of that, one has to want that more than anything else. One should desperately crave for that stellar position and be absolutely against any part of the self that accepts remaining anything less than 'Caesar'. 'For example' – writes Kierkegaard – 'when the ambitious man whose slogan is "Either Caesar or nothing" does not get to be Caesar, he despairs over it. But this also means something else: precisely because he did not get to be Caesar, he now cannot bear to be himself. Consequently, he does not despair because he did not get to be Caesar but despairs over himself [for being unable] to get to be Caesar.'[36] And in his inimitable, ironic style he goes on to explain: 'This self, which, if he had become Caesar, would have been in seventh heaven . . . this self is now utterly intolerable to him. In a deeper sense, it is not his failure to become Caesar that is intolerable, but it is this self that did not become Caesar that is intolerable; or, to put it even more accurately, what is intolerable to him is that he cannot get rid of himself. If he had become Caesar, he would despairingly get rid of himself, but he did not become Caesar and cannot despairingly get rid of himself.'[37] And to go along with Kierkegaard's logic we could ask, 'What if he actually became Caesar?' or 'Would he actually get rid of himself and be the self he would like to be?' 'Not quite,' would be Kierkegaard's reply, because he would be the sort of Caesar who has had to become Caesar not in order to be Caesar but to get rid of a self that felt like a worthless subject unless he became Caesar. In whichever way we try, the dialectics induces a vicious – and indeed perverse – circle of passivity.

In reflecting on the sort of pathology 'achieved' by individuals who are especially active, affirmative and successful, we can perhaps better appreciate the variegated problem of 'success'. And we should also consider those less omnipotent, benign cases in which we 'make a success' of our ordinary lives. Bollas's clinical remarks are illuminating in this sense. He draws attention to the exemplary partners of the conventional husband and wife dyad 'who do the right things in the right way at the appropriate time'.[38] And he asks if these conventions may have become insufferable restrictions and the inhibitors of any spontaneity. He also wonders whether conventional persons are *not* ultimately living their lives, although performing the convention to their best. 'Grotesque and unfair as it may seem, what if a divorced man, a family-opted-out woman, a career drop-out, or a maverick is an indicator of a move towards greater life usage?' And he concludes that to authentically live life, individuals should engage in a critical deconstruction of the conventions that are supportive but not ultimately enhancing.[39]

Still less omnipotent and more benign is 'busyness', which seems to partially substitute for spontaneity. The powerful 'compensators' speak and act as though 'being busy' is a force beyond their control, and they seem to be imprisoned within a lifestyle that is a breathless rush of activity. This sort of common behaviour is probably the expression of an inner psychic condition. We seem to adhere to an unspoken assumption that life must be busy, and that being busy is an indicator of social importance and success: a surplus of activity is equated with success. But then, choosing to resist the fixities of our role, however successful, seems to be a precondition for making any advances in the development of spontaneity. When action derives from imitative, discordant sources, such as the entitlement to compensation, we may even complain of not being 'seen' in spite of our busyness. But our complacent culture also provides instruments for 'solving' these problems by offering instruction and devices leading to visibility, to the certainty of an impact effect – because a powerful communicator can, of course, be more easily successful in the implementation of inner, unconscious projects. The predicament can be made even more intense inasmuch as successful 'agency' seems to easily lead to celebrity. And it seems that celebrity is in the nature of a general mania in our time. Celebrity, in fact, is positioned at the opposite end of passivity and shame, and it is celebrity that is often admired to the point of envy. And thus celebrity comes to appear as the most powerful antidote to the affliction of shameful passivity. If spontaneity is illusorily equated with the greater or lesser power to do as one pleases, then the 'spontaneity' of celebrities would also come to appear as an attribute to be coveted and possessed to the exclusion of all others. We might think that the power of celebrity could make one spontaneous in the sense that one can do as one wishes without bearing the burden of human negotiation. But then, this sort of perverse spontaneity would be ultimately dependent on the unconscious submissiveness of others, and it could only be gained at someone else's psychic expense.

Chapter 6

Actions and reactions

From the mechanics of reaction to the spontaneity of action

The prototype of reaction could be seen in the mechanism of splitting and projection which characterizes inchoative vicissitudes, while the prototype of psychic action can be regarded as an inner initiative which does not succumb to reactive mechanisms and which leads to paradox and creativity; it leads to a condition for action proper – action *for* something. Through reactions we illusorily 'think' that we may become free *from* something. Reactions share the characteristics of being quasi-'automatic', of being psychic mechanisms of remedy or revenge, of being non-responsible responses. We thus envisage a gradient between the two opposite poles of freedom-from and freedom-to.

Play, for instance, becomes possible only when creatures no longer respond automatically to another organism's behaviour but are able to communicate about the nature of their behaviour and about its context. This is what probably makes play the precursor of maturation and a milestone in the development of civilization. But, of course, we would like to understand what mental activity splits the mind apart; the problem, again, is that it is perhaps not so much an activity but a reactive attitude. The question remains as to which part of the mind actually 'does' the splitting–projecting move. As is known, the inchoate person not only responds to otherness but also responds to its instinctual propelling forces. Thus, reactive splitting could be seen as the effort to confront stimulus overload, object impingement or traumatic-level conflict by a defensive dissociation that seeks to establish internal mastery over external assault or instinctual threat. And yet, the fact that in psychoanalytic parlance we constantly refer to splitting and projective mechanisms seems to suggest that there must be some alternative and not-so-mechanical state where action proceeds from an integrated centre – but does not amount to a mechanism. We often describe the reactive condition as a deplorable[1] mental state that should be transformed into the potential for integrated psychic action, stemming from some agentive 'I'.

For the sake of clarification, we should perhaps move from a theoretical developmental perspective onto a more clinical outlook; the therapeutic approach, in fact, is the polar opposite of reaction: the analyst is the one who does not react. The essence of the technique is not only the renunciation of reaction for the sake of enhancing psychopoietic[2] action, but also the development of indirect action – as the principal condition for sustaining the opportunity for therapeutic work. The essence of the strategy is in fact indirect action. If we simply react, we may confine ourselves to playing the pathological games of the sufferers by their own rules. To describe the maintenance of the analytic attitude, Ury insists that the breakthrough strategy is 'indirect action'.[3] It requires the analyst to do the opposite of what one might feel like doing in challenging situations. When the interlocutor attacks, one may feel like escalating; confronted with hostility, one might retort; provoked by unreasonable requests, one may reject the entire relationship; when defied with rigidity, one may insist. These are the critical instances in which the therapeutic attitude upholds the essential difference between the simplicity of reaction and the complexity of psychic action.[4]

In the inevitable action–reaction gradient of human behaviour, the extreme end of reactivity could be expressed in accordance with Weil's essential remark to the effect that 'The tendency to spread suffering beyond ourselves almost functions like the force of gravity. If through excessive weakness we can neither elicit compassion nor do harm to others, we ultimately attack what the universe itself represents for us. Then every good or beautiful thing is like an insult.'[5] This general schema is to be somehow revealed for something to change. In between reactive behaviour – at one end of the scale – and psychopoietic actions – at the opposite end – there seems to be a distance that we cannot simply cross by means of any prefabricated device. Perhaps we can only 'leap' across this distance – continually, innumerable times. And every time, as we try to sprint, we are easily stricken by fear. Expressions such as 'bridging gaps', 'making connections', 'linking opposites' are too attractive and seductive. It is perhaps a question instead of a capacity for shifting and leaping. It all depends on the development of a basic attitude – the heart to make a venture – rather than on the production of instruments of whatever kind. It is a question of overcoming rigidity and advancing towards the sort of spontaneity that allows for psychic leaps. It sounds paradoxical to say that immediate reactions function in the domain of rigidity, while creative actions involve the capacity to leap into staying still, into waiting for the good inspiration.

Generally in life when anything is just beginning to go wrong, it is usually fairly easy to make corrections, as small adjustment is all that is needed. But it is sometimes hard at first to spot that there is any problem at all, such as an elusive inclination to reactivity. And if we have some inkling of the problem, it is not easy at such an early stage to define well what it is. In fact, the inchoate difficulty of generating psychopoietic actions, rather than merely indulging in reactions, often has to wait until the situation gets much worse; only then we can see what is wrong and what needs to be done to change it. In the logic of Oliver, subjectivity is experienced as the sense of agency and response-ability which develops through the unending encounter with otherness.[6] Agency is not an obligatory status, while response-ability is the capacity to actually respond with an action rather than a reaction. The reactive acts that have been done come into awareness through the instrumentality of their consequences. As soon as they come into awareness, they are felt and have to be borne, together with guilt and fear. It is for this reason that the emergence of authentic personhood is never smooth. Perhaps the first recorded case of reactive behaviour is that of Cain, being 'forced' to kill by his own envious reaction. An essential aspect of being a subject is the creative tolerance of one's own libidinal and aggressive features. An individual who systematically hates and obliterates the bad in himself is condemned to being, largely, a non-person.[7] One may even try to be an ideal without deficits of character, so that all the reactive projections are disowned into surrounding figures. In the forceful language of Weil, we could say that 'To be able to harm others with impunity – for instance to pass our anger onto an inferior who is obliged to be silent – is to spare ourselves from an expenditure of energy, an expenditure which the other person will have to make . . . [But then] the energy we economize in this way is immediately debased.'[8] But what is 'debased energy' if not a source of rigidity?

The kind of question about which most of us are in constant trouble is our understanding of the nature of our actions/reactions and of the reactions/actions of those around us. Our problems present us with an unnerving double vision as we try to use two different approaches in terms of either reactions or actions. We can explain reactions in purely causalistic terms, whereas in order to generate understandable actions we should be able to describe them in terms that make some kind of sense to the agents themselves – perhaps in terms of teleological, final causes. We wonder whether it is legitimate, in a culture where causalistic explanations are deeply respected and seem to claim omni-competence, to go on construing creative psychic action in the 'non-scientific' terms that allow us to understand from the inside, to understand in terms of inner motives – in a logic of teleology, intentionality and finality.[9] As we know, the adaptiveness and plasticity of action is designed precisely for the achievement of goals – however remote – in the face of variation and adversity; striving to achieve something seems required for its attainment. This is the context in which the notion of desire starts to work. Situations have a 'valency' for the living being according to whether they enhance or disrupt its integrity and capacity for action.[10] Perception of a state of affairs as being positive or negative in this sense is closely linked to some sort of valuational attitude. Thus, cognition and desire could ultimately be defined in terms of human acting, in the sense that cognition serves action by processing information, and desire signifies the point and motive of it all. But these functions are interwoven aspects of one process: the goals of action have to be cognitively represented and its methods must have an affective aim. From this perspective, desire has cognitive structure and content, while cognition operates at the service of achieving aims – and hence involves desire. We can thus adopt the general hypothesis that affects are cognitive and cognition is affectual. Conversely, the production of a well-formed syntax could be seen as having no point except itself, just like the information exchange between mathematically defined systems. In this sense they can be said to perform tasks, even though they actually don't mind whether they achieve them or not. So the ideas of a task as well as of success are ours rather than theirs – our psychic action, indeed. Reactions are comparable to the automatic functions of computers in the sense that the final successful goal seems secondary or irrelevant with respect to the immediacy of a reaction; this is a response to a propelling 'fire' and not at all strategically oriented towards success. We could even say that, paradoxically, angry, reactive subjects do not seem to care whether they succeed or not.

Anger and reactions

As we gradually realize that we are 'responsible' for our psychic life, we can begin to be capable of action. Before that, we primarily react. And anger, of course, could be seen as one of the most conspicuous examples of reactive behaviour. A person only becomes aware of reactive activity when he has achieved some subjective agency by means of integrative development. The maturational process makes it possible for us to become aware of the rigidity of reactions. For, in fact, these distinctions ultimately allow us to consider the effect of our behaviour upon the self. The obscured side – or the 'Shadow side', as Jung would call it – can only be seen when silhouetted against the light of action proper, of creative action.

Symington reiterates that the resentful act generates madness, while the act of acceptance creates sanity.[11] There is a profound difference between those two acts: one is reactive, whereas the other is a personal creation. The hateful act could be considered primarily instinctive, while the accepting attitude we would regard as personal and creative. Thus, the ability to decide, choose and create are the prime manifestations of sanity. The individual who is acting sanely is the one who can think rather than just react. A thought is an inner action, concludes Symington[12] – as would, of course, Bion. The person is constituted of an array of disparate attitudes, all of which are taken up in the creative act of acceptance. Self-acceptance thus appears as a precursor of acceptance, as a uniquely personal creation. It is this very pristine creative attitude that shapes the ego. In a more Darwinian perspective, however, one could also say that we are all naturally angry: anger is natural, and perhaps even healthy. We need anger to right wrongs, to revolt against oppression. In a naturalistic outlook on human life we might claim that we are 'hardwired' with anger. We probably need it to protect ourselves from the danger of aggression or oppression; perhaps it is our source of courage in fight. And yet we retrospectively see anger as a quasi-automatic, unexplainable response that can dominate both ourselves *and* others. Thurman remarks that 'You may be gripped by fight or flight reactions, you may practically need to defend yourselves and have no time to feel sorry for your delusional attacker'; and then he concludes, 'but why bother to explode in anger?'[13]

When one is not spontaneous, doing nothing out of one's own will – *sua sponte* – it is almost natural for the person to cause some harm to others. So we need not waste energy getting angry with the non-spontaneous subjects when they are hurtful to us, and we could just make every effort to minimize or avoid harm. In Thurman's view, the problem with anger is that it erroneously focuses on some putative intentional agency of the person who causes damage: 'You absolutize that agency as ill-intentioned . . . and only then does your anger explode to destroy that enemy. But now that you know the other person is helplessly the tool of his own anger . . . then you can only be angry with the mental addiction that drives him. . . . Anger is only destroyed by not getting angry! Effective anger at anger can only become the energy of tolerance.'[14] We do not, of course, have a 'hatred' of natural elements, however violent they may be. Yet, our production of enemies is probably based on our projecting an independent subjective agency into a being that 'chooses' to damage us. As analysts we can fairly easily appreciate how the enemy is basically an automaton comparable to a natural phenomenon whose behaviour is passively driven by unconscious impulses and attitudes – just like our own when we indulge in angry reactions. The other may have no independence of will, no capacity to act *sua sponte*, and may be the helpless victim of his own passivity, operating mechanically and without intentionality. The pathology of the other lacks personal agency that intends us harm, and so we have no real target for the sort of rage that could consciously select the source of our suffering and so regain well-being by destroying it. In an eloquent synoptic view, Thurman remarks that 'Mundane heroes who fight and kill other beings are themselves fuelled by anger, are the minions of anger, and they slay zombie-like bodies of enemies who themselves are but tools of anger. . . . You are a corpse of a hero killing corpses, both of you defeated by the real enemy, anger.'[15] A comparable outlook on human agency has been incisively expressed in Weil's writings, especially in her chapters on 'Imagination Which Fills the Void', 'Illusions' and 'Violence'. In a nutshell: 'Monotony of evil: never anything new, everything about it is *equivalent*. Never anything real, everything about it is imaginary.'[16]

To the extent that anger is metabolized through psychoanalytic work, its energy can be saved, and it can still be there for us to use in a detoxified form, for destructive drives cannot just be eliminated, of course. Their 'furious fire' can perhaps – hopefully – be used in a creative way. The energy used so destructively by anger can thus become free, at least in part, for creative purposes. Freud clearly contends that indeed libidinal energy could even exist in a desexualized form, as a unifying force holding the self together. He says: 'The enlarged sexuality of psychoanalysis coincides with the love of the divine Plato.'[17] Not dissimilarly, the destructive energy of anger could also exist in a manageable form, in the form of a force intended for impact on the outside world. Anger seems some ultimate psychic 'fire', and compassion could perhaps use this fire with effectiveness to diminish the suffering of other beings.[18] Ideally, psychoanalytic work should generate a development whereby we are freed from being the tools and become the managers of our deep energies.

Thurman writes that 'When before it seemed that you must be angry at what really is too much to bear, now you are enabled to be patient and more capable in perceiving and responding, since you can see things external and internal from many other angles.'[19] But then, when we say that the harmfulness of the other is phantasmal, reactive, mechanical, we refer to the quality of the way in which it exists, and this does not at all mean that it is nonexistent; it does remain harmful. Our insight, however, makes for a much better preparedness.

From the clinician's perspective, one can begin to find more abundant 'happiness' by forging ways of using common causes of suffering into motives for psychic growth; one can then use frustrating experiences to develop ego strengths and capacities for paradox. Thus oriented towards spontaneity, the mind can renounce superficial pleasures in the quest for reliable inner health. Ideally, the plentiful causes of suffering could provide plentiful reasons for reliable inner health. But then, crucial problems remain. Even as 'adults' we fear that suffering may ultimately destroy us; as infants, of course, we only gradually prepare for maturation on condition that circumstances prove ultimately tolerable. Kristeva remarks that however distressing, unbearable or exhilarating it may be, our psychic life allows us access to other people; 'Because of the soul, you are capable of action. Your psychic life is a discourse that acts. Whether it harms you or saves you, you are its subject.' And she concludes: 'We cannot dispense with a teleonomy here.'[20] From the mechanics of reaction we can move all the way to a sort of 'detachment from the fruits of action',[21] in the language of Weil; to act not for a purpose but from creative 'necessity', actually from spontaneity. Although it is laboriously developed, once we 'reach' spontaneity we may not exactly know the motives of our action. Once we are acting spontaneously, we cannot be proud of what we do, even though we might accomplish marvels.

As Eigen suggests, therapy may help the analysand process injury and rage and help broaden one's response repertoire to the incitement of anger; an evolution in processing ability and response capability is authentic maturation. But he also points out that the evolution of the ability to live decently with the vast unprocessable parts of the self – including wounds that never heal – is of *equal* importance.[22] Analysis is commonly regarded as a transformational endeavour. But perhaps more than actual change, what is developed is a greater attitude of spontaneity in the sense of both initiative *and* acceptance. It can be exhausting to monotonously react to alarming inner or outer 'circumstances'. In fact, those who are seriously ill cannot work – perform actions – because they are already deprived of energy by their constant 'work' – that is, by having to constantly react. The possibility of actual work would be a restorative experience. But then, since some of us may actually *want* to act on impulse – that is, to simply react – without feeling guilty, we seek some accredited authority to endorse our impulses.[23] The person who is summoned to act as the inspiring authority might even complacently come to believe that he is extremely important to that person, whereas he is actually controlled and put at the leash by the 'humble' and rageful seeker of advice. The person who refuses the role of the omniscient guru actually refuses to comply with the rigidity of the patient's reactive attitude. Conversely, the analyst might even enter into a collusion. Acting on impulse eschews pain and difficulty, whereas acting spontaneously involves endurance and responsibility. In fact, the reactive creature may only harm others as a way of complying with his own 'therapeutic' scheme, however futile. How is that for a psychic paradox? From still another paradoxical outlook, Weil suggests that if someone injures me, I must ensure that his injury will not degrade me; and I must desire this outcome out of *respect* for the one who has inflicted it in order that he may not have done any harm, really.[24] But then, this is possible to the extent that we may regularly enjoy action more than reaction.

Chapter 7

The question of forgiveness

Our ordinary genius

The 'creative genius' on which we intend to focus here is not the acclaimed creativity of art and science, but the essential creativity of our daily psychic efforts aimed at survival, coexistence, empathy and forgiveness. If creativity is opted for, it usually becomes a principle of action within the self: it comes into being within inner life in the attitude of choosing and desiring it. A lack of creativeness indicates that pressured activity derives from a situation where the contingencies of the self are detached from the deeper sources of psychic life. And, in fact, the prevalence of reactions, as contrasted with the action of developing paradoxes, somehow induces an atrophy of inner life. According to Winnicott, when psychoanalysis has attempted to explore the issue of creativity it has largely lost sight of its main theme: 'The creative impulse is . . . something that is present when *anyone* – baby, child, adolescent, adult, old man or woman – looks in a healthy way at anything or *does anything deliberately*.'[1] In relational events of any kind, there is always space for some extra sublimation that leads to creativity, to genius, to the extraordinary in the life of ordinary people. According to Oliver, even in adverse circumstances the extraordinary surplus within the routine, the virtuoso performance, gradually decolonizes psychic space and liberates it from the restrictions of tradition. She remarks, nevertheless, that the possibility of sublimation and creativity can be missing from the lives of 'marginalized people insofar as they are circumscribed by values, meanings and images that foreclose their agency as meaning makers'.[2] And yet it is this basic insistence on any kind of minimal forms of creativity that opens routes towards the creation of ulterior meaning. Oliver also remarks that geniuses are necessary inspirations for our psychic life: inner life depends on a sense of legitimization of the possibility of creativity and greatness for all of us.[3] But to practise idealization and identification, we also need to conceive of genius as the product of the life of ordinary people who do simple but extraordinary things.

With this outlook we can appreciate that psychoanalytic work often encourages us to realize that the expression of genius might really lie more in the search than in the attainment, in the creative process rather than in its end result. The idealizations by which we value the end result more than the process lead us unrealistically to expect some fulfilment that is completely free from any inhibition, ambivalence or limit – that is, a product of unalloyed genius. But perhaps the idealizations and denials conducive to the putative state of total creativeness are sustained by means of projections of one's narcissistic fantasies and grandiose images. The idealization may so devalue the process of attainment that it becomes purely instrumental, something to be marginalized and regarded as valueless with respect to the acclaimed end result; in being valueless, it is exploited at the utmost while also looked upon as a dehumanized, mechanical part of one's life. In this sense, idealizations conspire to undermine any creative process whatsoever, as if one were compelled to always act in light of some procrastinated sort of success. And yet, our ordinary human genius does not procrastinate – no matter what current, ordinary circumstances can allow for our daily expressions of genius.

Kristeva and Howe describe 'the' genius as a subject who lives at a cultural intersection and crystallizes its possibilities; but they also maintain that genius belongs to all of us as a 'therapeutic invention' by which we create and live; it is the capacity to imagine the extraordinary within our ordinary lives.[4] We may, in fact, be afraid that the quality of genius will be diminished or banalized if we remove the magic and mystery surrounding it. But geniuses 'simply' show us what humankind is capable of. And according to Howe, 'it is only when we acknowledge that geniuses are not totally unlike other people that our minds open up to all that we can learn from them'.[5] Genius inspires us to maximize our capacities and gives us a sense not only of what we lack, but of what we can ordinarily do. Of course, creativity requires sublimation, and this is commonly available to all of us. In Oliver's view, genius provides the inspiration that ordinary people can use to speak *through* the clichés of culture as individuals who belong to that culture as singular, different beings.[6] This is the often unrecorded everyday genius of those who manage to speak with their singular, unique voices. But our ordinary genius is not a fixed, steady pattern, of course, and it expresses itself by means of cycles, fluctuations and rhythms. In Bollas' view, in fact, 'Psychic life during an ordinary day . . . is an endless sequence of psychic intensities and their subsequent fragmentations. This process – of collecting condensations which in turn serve as the material of disseminative scattering – is vital to the individual unconscious creativity in living.'[7] Bollas also specifies that though the dream process is perhaps a way of appreciating our unconscious freedom, the same process can also occur to some degree in our daily experiences, whenever we conjure ideas from the unity of our embodied condition.[8] These experiences are moments of psychic intensity –

indeed, expressions of our ordinary human genius. In Eigen's synoptic view, the concerns of Bion, Lacan and Winnicott basically 'converge on a central interest: creative experiencing, what makes it possible or hinders it (formally and descriptively). They chart detailed ways in which creative experiencing involves paradox, mystery or faith expressed through dialectical thinking. In effect, each tries to develop something of a phenomenology of creative experiencing.'[9]

If we conceive of alienation – the most pervasive pathology of our times – as an essential lack of creativity, we could see it as the source of modern malaise; in this connection Symington dares to say: 'That narcissism cuts us from our own creative source of action, I am sure. That our job is to repair our own minds, I am sure. That true creative action provides the occasion for new harmonies in society, I am sure. Our first task is to harness our potential for creative action. Once we do this, our symptoms and pathology will subside.'[10]

The genius of forgiveness

In Arendt we read that 'In contrast to revenge, which is the natural, automatic reaction to transgression and which . . . can be expected and even calculated – the act of forgiving can never be predicted; it is the only reaction that acts in an unexpected way and thus retains, though being a reaction, something of the original character of action. Forgiveness, in other words, is the only reaction which does not merely re-act but acts anew and unexpectedly . . . frees from its consequences both the one who forgives and the one who is forgiven.'[11] Not only Arendt but also Weil, Kristeva, Derrida and Oliver have in various ways regarded forgiveness as a threshold of humanity. They seem to converge in saying that to be human is to be capable of forgiving. If forgiveness is essential to human life, and more specifically to the development of subjective agency, then, as Oliver suggests, 'the absence of forgiveness undermines humanity, subjectivity and agency'.[12] Most psychoanalytic models posit a primary conflict between the individual and the social order that is constitutive of subjectivity. Oliver argues that it is not alienation or struggle but, rather, forgiveness that is constitutive of subjectivity as understood in a new and more realistic/pragmatic way. She develops a psychoanalytic social theory of forgiveness as an alternative – or, perhaps, an integration – of both philosophical and psychoanalytic notions of subjectivity as based on struggle with, and alienation from, the world.[13]

We often think of creativity and genius in terms of unique works in the domain of art and science. But probably a more relevant expression of creative genius is our human capacity to generate relationships, such as the critical and essential relation of forgiveness; this requires a genius for creating unforeseeable developments. We could invoke here Winnicott's conviction that 'The creativity that concerns me here is a universal. It belongs to being alive. . . . The creativity that we are studying belongs to the approach of the individual to external reality.'[14] It is in fact the extraordinary within the ordinary, in the language of Kristeva. Genius is the inner attitude of ordinary people who do extraordinary minimal things – and thus do not comply. In Winnicott's view, compliance carries with it a sense of futility and is associated with the idea that nothing matters and that life is not worth living: 'In a tantalizing way many individuals have experienced just enough of creative living to recognize that for most of their time they have been living uncreatively. . . . These two alternatives of living creatively or uncreatively can be very sharply contrasted.'[15] From this outlook, genius gives us a sense not of what we lack but of what we can become. An appreciation of the genius of forgiveness is all the more urgent because it shows us the extraordinary of our humanity beyond automation and standardization. Metaphorically speaking, it points in the direction of depth rather than magnitude. Given the way that social movement is circumscribed within certain patriarchal cultures or oppressive communities, it could be said that the psychic space of certain individuals who do not have power is 'deep', and that the inner space of more powerful members is 'vast'.[16] Spontaneity and healing have less to do with the amplitude of our minds and more to do with the potential for depth, for seeking our unknown, unthinkable resources, such as even the ultimate capacity to pity one's oppressors and to forgive neglect and abuse. This is in fact the unplumbable quality that is present in our genius of forgiveness. Parsons remarks that 'An idea, a perception, the expression of feeling in a turn of phrase – all sorts of *everyday* things may suddenly, apparently out of the blue, show us ourselves and the world in a new light. These moments of illumination may be slight or epiphanic. Seeming to come from nowhere, they come from nowhere but within ourselves and . . . give us the sense of a *deep* internal process, part of ourselves and strange to us at the same time.'[17] From a different but converging perspective, Berlin suggests that 'We ought to seek the knowledge that is involved when a piece of work is described *not* as correct or incorrect, skilful or inept, a success or a failure, but as profound or shallow, . . . perceptive or stupid, alive or "dead".'[18]

Geniuses are necessary for psychic life; we need them to validate the exceptional within our lives: 'Psychic life depends on a sense of validation and legitimation of the possibility of creativity and greatness for all of us.'[19] But in order to use idealization for identification, we also need to reconceive of genius as the product of the most ordinary people who do extraordinary things in the most ordinary and obscure of interpersonal dynamics. In the language of Winnicott: 'It is not of course that anyone will ever be able to explain the creative impulse . . . but the link can be made, and usefully made, between creative living and living itself'[20] – that is, living our ordinary lives. In Oliver's view, the idea of genius is an antidote to degrading stereotypes that impair psychic space and the movements of drives towards signification.[21] Genius provides the inspiration that allows ordinary people to speak, even *through* the degrading clichés of a culture. Of course, there are expressions of genius that are documented in our cultural heritage; but then, there can be innumerable acts of genius that are not in the least bit recorded or appreciated. This is the everyday genius of ordinary people, which often only speaks to the singularity of another individual. We are only interested here in these inconspicuous, silent, germinative forms of genius. And we can be aware of these unassuming, daily expressions of genius even though we cannot properly theorize them.

One of the features of maturation and therapy is that we become able to express our aggressive desires through cultural codes, rather than acting them out; giving voice to these violent desires, however, presupposes a cultural dimension of forgiveness. This dimension may be quite tacit and unspoken. Instead of all experience being based on a unitary form of public knowledge, we could envisage a spectrum of experience ranging from the articulate to the unspoken. From a cultural perspective, only the genius of forgiveness enables revolt, by enhancing a transfer of affects and drives into a more articulate signification. In this connection, Oliver remarks that 'although forgiveness is not the product of one consciousness forgiving the other, it is dialogic in the sense that it happens between two communicating bodies, two bodies mediated by meaning, or what in psychoanalytic discourse we have come to call "the third". The agency of forgiveness is the operation of this third that should not be attributed to either one party or the other. Rather, the agency of forgiveness is the effect of meaning.'[22]

The labour of forgiveness

The potential for reason to improve our lives is, perhaps, hampered by an imbalance due to theoretical rigidity. We thus need to confront the challenges of an uncertain human world not with inflexible theories, but through a more humane and compassionate form of psychic exploration, one that accepts the complexity and variability that is our psychic life as an essential beginning of inquiry. Ideally reconnecting both this problem and the creative labours of forgiveness, Wittgenstein remarks that 'The *important* fine shades of behaviour are not predictable.'[23] From a perspective of flexibility, we can better appreciate that the revolt that is essential to genius ultimately presupposes a cultural atmosphere of forgiveness   that is, the possibility of negotiating between singularity and universality, contingency and innovation. Oliver insists that 'Forgiveness is the counterweight to alienated individuals at odds with others.'[24] But then again, only forgiveness can ultimately resolve the *debilitating* condition of being at odds with the world – with the others. In fact, if one can be so personally agentive as to arrive at the level of forgiveness, then one can also be sufficiently active as to freely make a promise. The genius of forgiveness is expressed in a double action of unbinding: the pardoned individual disengages himself from the enduring results of offence, and by pardoning the other he disengages the offender from his own actions. This same active force, moreover, truly enables us to make promises – that is, binding our agency not only to the present relations but also to future circumstances. With exemplary parsimony of words, Arendt describes our genius of forgiveness as an eminently object-related experience: 'The moral code inferred from the faculty of forgiving . . . rests on experiences which nobody could ever have with himself, which, on the contrary, are entirely based on the presence of others.'[25]

Although forgiveness supports the development of subjects, this is not the policy of a sovereign will. Oliver reiterates that 'Psychoanalytic forgiveness is forgiveness without sovereignty, forgiveness beyond recognition.'[26] Psychoanalysis in fact forges forgiveness as an essential 'third way'. In the language of Kristeva, 'Forgiveness makes it possible to become a subject without murdering the other or dejecting or abjecting oneself. . . . At the extreme, rather than kill we confess our desire to kill; and this confession requires, that is, presupposes, forgiveness.'[27] The sort of parental love that does not irradiate forgiveness can be a caricature of love. Symington suggests that idealizing love can be experienced as a rejection of one's spontaneity inasmuch as that part of the self that possessively desires the parent is inevitably rejected.[28] The jealous little Oedipus who tries to conquer the mother is essentially rejected, and thus parental love can be a trap; love of this sort is not life-enhancing as it does not really accept the desirous, aggressive creature. Oliver theorizes that both the revolt and sublimation necessary for psychic life presuppose forgiveness – not the forgiveness from a sovereign agent but, rather, forgiveness as a social dynamic that generates both sovereignty and individuality.[29] Without an atmosphere of forgiveness, those who do not feel forgiven may, of course, refuse to identify with a persecutory authority and act in a contrary direction, ultimately in the sense of a spiteful reaction and not quite in the form of spontaneous action. In the vicissitudes of transference, the analysand projects his inner oppressors onto the analyst and at the same time actively absorbs an experience of acceptance that enables him to 'forgive' his internalized oppressive objects. And so we could say that according to the worst hypothesis one identifies with them and perpetuates their behaviour; to a better hypothesis, we re-act to their oppression and behave in the opposite way; to an even better hypothesis, one actually acquits inner and outer oppressors and thus reaches the level of creative, psychopoietic actions – which are no longer simple reactions, not in the least – they are expressions of genius.

The labour of forgiveness as the act of unbinding, and the capacity to make promises as the work of binding, are perhaps insufficiently explored from a psychoanalytic perspective. In fact, what the suffering subject disapproves of is neglect and abuse, but what he rages against is a parental figure. The incapacity to forgive perpetuates an inner rigidity that prevents empathy and makes hostility compulsory. Thus, the absence of forgiveness translates into continued hatred of inner and outer objects. But then, what we actually observe in psychoanalytic vicissitudes is that hatred ultimately weighs on the person who is captured and exhausted by it; in this sense he cannot afford the inner force to bind himself into a creative promise. The insufficiently good parent could be envisaged as the one who cannot truly forgive. The good-enough patient is the one who refuses to simply inherit this attitude, and ultimately does forgive. By doing so his actions are no longer reactions to internalized abjecting others, but actions proper, spontaneous actions. Ideally, analysis is the way to break this repetitive script. The genius of forgiveness functions on the basis of a laboriously developed capacity for mentally separating the agent and the action: one can untie oneself from primal relational vicissitudes to the extent that one can also untie primal others from their decried behaviour. Paradoxically, this form of splitting is an act of genius, a total novelty, a credit conferred to our own potential for regeneration. Difficult but not impossible, it is certainly envisionable. But then, the creative labour of forgiveness is no 'happy ending' genre. No, it is a never-ending psychopoietic, maturational, challenging story.

As clinicians know well, cumulative rage helps nourish a pessimistic, depressive, semi-malevolent undertow to one's official, happier self. According to Eigen, bitterness is closer to the surface in some people, while in others it works more silently.[30] One may recoil with surprise at the bitter rage that a nice person harbours. In either case, chronic outrage over injury can erode inner life and our creative potential. Eigen contends that latent, explosive hatred obliterates the self. In contrast to an asphyxiating inner atmosphere of bitterness and rage, Arendt points out that a climate of forgiveness 'is the exact opposite of vengeance, which acts in the form of reacting against an original trespassing, whereby far from putting an end to the consequences of the first misdeed, everything remains bound to the process, permitting the chain reaction contained in every action to take its unhindered course'.[31] This sadly perpetuates an asphyxiating atmosphere. If hatred tends to make us blind with respect to our objects, then in the long run it will paralyse our capacities for insight and also reduce our inner depths. Our essential priority will be the development of a clear assessment of the blinding powers of hatred – both suffered and activated. This clarity on the consequences of hatred will certainly contribute to a condition of better preparedness.

An excessive level of 'fear of castration' can be the phantasmal equivalent of tragic consequences; this terror is probably of no use for the wonderful developments and achievements generally attributed to the Oedipal turn. Conversely, Oedipal vicissitudes are maturationally significant to the extent that an atmosphere of forgiveness is culturally available. Fear of retaliation in itself and by itself could turn out to be maturationally futile. The question is what happens in the developing self when Oedipal vicissitudes prove impassable because of an excess of threat and a scary milieu created by parental figures who are incapable of forgiveness. The developing person may be induced to retreat from the triadic paradigm back into the more primitive dyadic relation. Under these circumstances, the individual cannot learn from an experience of forgiveness and cannot count on the cultural openings deriving from the Oedipal passage. Under these adverse conditions, a surplus of genius is required in order not to identify with the parental figures and thus disengage oneself from such asphyxiating paradigms. The thesis here is that it is not the fear of castration that is the ultimate propeller of the Oedipal passage but, rather, the possible experience of forgiveness. From a more social perspective, Oliver remarks that colonization and oppression operate by attacking subjectivity and agency, foreclosing the possibility of sublimation: 'It is forgiveness . . . – the agency of meaning or signification – that makes sublimation and idealization possible . . ., it is the suspension of judgement or presupposition of forgiveness before judgement that instigates and sustains subjectivity.'[32] In the absence of an atmosphere of forgiveness, the developing subject will forever try to react to harsh social figures and persecutory internal objects – perhaps even trying to behave in the opposite way. And so when an attitude of forgiveness is not internalized, there will always be reactions rather than actions and the maturational journey may remain incomplete. It may take a surplus of genius, in fact, to attempt forgiveness in a relational milieu in which it has not been experienced: when forgiveness is attempted, it is truly an act of revolutionary genius.

In a synoptic view of the labour of forgiveness, Oliver reiterates that asserting individuality is a trespass against the social, a trespass that requires cultural acquittal to forge our sense of belonging. It is not trespass but, rather, acquittal that is definitive of both individuality and community. And this is not to say, according to Oliver, that there is any sovereign agent of forgiveness; on the contrary, the agency of social forgiveness is meaning itself, which in turn produces the effect of sovereignty.[33] It is not that social forgiveness presupposes a sovereign agent but, rather, that forgiveness is a prerequisite for sovereignty.

Social implications

Theorists of forgiveness such as Weil, Arendt, Kristeva, Derrida and Oliver have in various ways made forgiveness a threshold of humanity: to be human is to forgive. If forgiveness is essential to human life, and more specifically to subjective agency, then, conversely, the absence of forgiveness may undermine this critical potential. As is known, according to Freud the ability to sublimate drives and their manifestations is the source of human civilization and creativity. Psychic life depends on the discharge of drives and affects into signification. Sublimation, however, presupposes a cultural context sufficiently hospitable to transformations – for vindictiveness and retribution, in fact, prevent any such transformative processes. It is thus rather puzzling that the idea of forgiveness is not specifically developed in Freud's work. According to Oliver, the colonization – as contrasted with the cultivation – of psychic space operates through withholding forgiveness. Colonization is, in fact, not development; it is primarily occupation for the sake of diverse forms of exploitation. She specifies that the lack of social space induced by colonization not only prevents the articulation of the painful and negative affects of oppression, but also undermines the possibility of sublimation.[34] The lack of forgiveness for the expression of drives and the silencing of personal affects create a type of double or even triple bind for those othered through a process of colonization. The result is that those othered by an oppressive and unforgiving culture are made to feel ashamed for their attempts to overcome subjection and for attempting sublimation; at the same time, they are forced to carry the burden of shame for instincts on behalf of the privileged ones – that is, carry it for those who project their own shame in order to benefit from the abjection of others. We could take 'abjection' to indicate a malignant form of passivity in the sense of self-dislike, self-oppression and self-degradation. If true revolution is one stemming from the depths of inspiration, this requires not only the creation of positive values extracted from personal depths, but also the revaluation of values, such that the very structure of valuation is opened up for transformation. It would be a transformation that may legitimately include the value of forgiveness. There are, indeed, multiple demands for those abjected by whatever forms of colonization or dominant ontologies prevail. On the social side, it requires throwing off not only the cultural or patriarchal imaginary chains but also the chains that bind the inner imagination and impede a growth in psychic depth, where the ultimate inner resources originate. And so the quality of inner space that is conducive to spontaneity cannot be described with the metaphor of magnitude but, rather, with the metaphor of depth. In a 'vast' mind, psychic resources may be abundant but homogeneous and vulnerable to being sequestered by colonization. In a 'deep' mind, they can be scarce but highly diversified and accurately concealed – to the point of even including a potential for compassion and forgiveness. If the colonized cannot forgive the colonizers, then they reproduce the abjective, unforgiving attitude of the colonizers, who drastically condemn in order to then use and abuse. The perverse form of attachment perpetrated by the colonizing agent is perpetuated by the person who is resourceful enough for contrary action – which amounts to a reaction – but who does not seek at a sufficient depth the unheard of resources for forgiving oppression.

To recapitulate Oliver's arguments, the maturation work for those excluded in any 'racist' way is doubly laborious because the subjects must seek forgiveness not only for their natural attempts to trespass, but also for their putative abject nature. The marginalized ones are 'made ashamed of what is deemed their abject difference'; and their 'evil' cannot be forgiven because it supposedly contaminates the purity of humanity.[35] Those who are not 'impure' can rejoin the social structure as those who belong, even after the trespass through which they assert their singular individuality. The abjected ones must cope not only with their attempt to reach subjectivity, but also with their preliminary condition that forecloses subjectivity. This itinerary is particularly laborious – and in a way a work of genius – because it demands the sort of 'trespass that transforms the very law that it breaks'; it requires a 'revolt that opens the law onto otherness and transforms it from cruel superego into forgiveness, which in turn enables the transformation of shame into agency'.[36] But then, in Arendt's view, both 'colonizers' and 'colonized' can benefit from the genius of forgiveness in the sense that it offers an escape from the pathologic severity of repetition. In fact, without being released from the consequences of what we have done, 'our capacity to act would . . . be confined to one single deed from which we could never recover; we could remain the victims of its consequences *forever*, not unlike the sorcerer's apprentice who lacked the magic formula to break the spell'.[37] In the language of Arendt, the banality of oppression is a resentful, impersonal deficit turning aggressive colonization into indifference. From this outlook, hatred is the projection of deficits; it is the sort of vindictiveness that is as terrible as it is impersonal and banal. And she concludes that 'The possible redemption from the predicament of irreversibility – of being unable to undo what one has done . . . – is the faculty of forgiving. . . . Forgiving serves to undo the deeds of the past, whose "sins" hang, like Damocles' sword, over every new generation.'[38]

Chapter 8

The quest for responsibility

The genius of responsibility

When things go wrong there is often a propensity to talk about bad luck, and in that way we seek to eschew any sense of responsibility for whatever happened. When things go extremely well, however, fewer seem inclined to talk about their good luck – unless, of course, they have advisers instructing them to do so. The thesis here is that a 'sufficient' sense of responsibility is essential for personhood and, also, that it is the critical element for healing and creativity.

If we regard scriptures as indicators of the psychology of a culture, we could read an instructive story dramatized in *Genesis*: the story of a creature who seeks to become a deity by means of a short cut or of a simple trick such as eating a piece of fruit. The fragile creature does not, in fact, try to become god-like through the innumerable ways of human ingenuity and creative action. But the significant psychological aspect of the whole situation is that he does not even own up to his attempt to use an expedient: the whole venture is simply not his responsibility. In his view there are at least three culprits: the lady with him, the God who put the lady next to him, and the serpent who enticed the lady. This is the weakness of our primordial father: a lack of creative agency, a lack of response-ability and no sense of an 'I' that, perhaps, could have attempted or not attempted to use a trick.

Although psychoanalytic culture acknowledges the effect of interpersonal influences on the psyche, it rarely indicates that interpersonal conditions actually become *constrictive* of psychic life. Subjectivity is regarded as the sense of agency and response-ability constituted in the encounter with otherness; it is the capacity to respond more or less freely, the freedom to actually respond with a psychic action – as contrasted with the simple reaction of disowning agency. Once responsibility is sacrificed in favour of some anaesthetized indifference, the opportunities for psychic life seem to close like a valve, impeding an inversion of currents. A desire for spontaneity seems to surface at whatever level we may be struggling to maintain life open to development and growth. The 'mentally ill' appear unable to be creative for themselves and others, even in favourable circumstances; rather, they tend to create rigidity and ambiguity. This tendency seems to depend on a psychic incompetence to deal with one's own incompetence in performance – that is, an incompetence to face personal incompetence.[1] The 'mentally healthy' could be described as able to generate creativity for themselves and others in spite of difficult and unfavourable conditions. This seems to depend on a psychological competence to accept one's incompetence, and to assume responsibility for it as a genuine starting point. And yet, nothing seems to compete with the attractiveness of whatever anaesthetizes us against responsibility. Anaesthetizers give us dispensation from taking care of our own self.

In our incapacity for responsibility, we seem to indirectly claim that our mental apparatus is not inhabited, not circumscribed, and cannot be interrogated. At the other extreme of our capacity to respond, we could envisage a situation describable in Bion's language as 'debris, remnants or scraps of imitated speech and histrionic synthetic emotion, floating in a space so vast that its confines, temporal as well as spatial, are without definition'.[2] As the felt recognition of intentionality, our sense of responsibility can accept defeat but not absurdity, can cope with meaningful adverse vicissitudes but not with meaningless circumstances. Responsibility is more significant and relevant than we are prepared to appreciate. As we frequently talk about reactions, imitations, anaesthetizing manoeuvres, all of this seems to suggest that there must be alternative modes of inner life where responsible action proceeds from some innermost part of a sufficiently integrated self. Moreover, the obscure, irresponsible attitude can only be seen when profiled against the light. Sanity is associated with the state of affairs where there is a responsible centre. But perhaps even mental illness is compatible with responsibility in the sense that a creative centre is there to at least endure, or cope with, a pathology that cannot be resolved. In Symington's view, the creative act can only occur when all parts of the self are contained within an encircling 'membrane'. When parts of the self are roaming around in figures and institutions – in our favourite bearers of responsibility – it is not possible to create: 'When envy, jealousy, and greed are tolerated and accepted as items in the personality, they cease to liquefy or petrify but instead endow the personality with strength.'[3]

Freud suggests that the psychoanalyst analyses, but the synthetic function – that is, the function whereby parts become integrated – is provided by the patient. This is the analysand's own response: elements are not expelled but are repossessed and put together. Through analysis 'The great unity which we call the ego fits into itself all the instinctual impulses which before had been split off and held apart from it', remarks Freud – rather hopefully.[4] And also, 'The psycho-synthesis is thus achieved during analytic treatment without our intervention, automatically and inevitably', he concludes even more hopefully.[5] But the essential question is how can we achieve this synthesis, and why we may fail to create it. This question is rarely asked. And yet it is quite central to traditional forms of culture that there is an intentional kernel that originates from within the living being; in most cultures, there is in fact a reward for acting in one way rather than another. By contrast, an oversimplified instinctual theory may imply that we are driven by quasi-alien forces. This is, of course, a paradox that we must accept as a problematic companion in our inquiry. In 'Lines of Advance in Psycho-Analytic Therapy', Freud insists that 'You can analyze the elements inside a person but the actual job of bringing them together and making something, that's nothing to do with the analyst' – and he refers to this as the 'synthetic function'.[6] It is an operation of conscience, a responsibility to draw in different parts and make them into a whole. By contrast, the ignorance of responsibility could be described as a condition of being strangers to ourselves, detached from a unifying centre. And the feeling of being removed from one's self, or dispersed into external projections – our celebrated 'alienation' – cannot simply be accounted for as the psychic residue of a problematic society. Cultural explanations seem good ones, but certainly not good enough, because the individual seems to reside somewhere in peripheral, semi-external psychic areas. In fact, we could also say that the person is the victim of an epistemological tradition whereby we illusorily posit and require that 'true' rationality be definitely detached from our personal affective life.[7]

Freedom-from and freedom-to

Humans have gained enormously in some areas of modern culture in the way of freedom *from* ignorance, *from* social oppression, *from* illness. The gains, however, are comparatively scarce in the domain of freedom *to* exercise creativity and *to* assume responsibility. Freedom-from could be considered as generically achieved, while freedom-to remains the ongoing problem of developing our ordinary genius. From a social perspective, we could say that freedom from adverse external factors is largely attainable, or at least we know how to go about seeking it. We, in fact, actively endeavour to be free from oppression, hunger and illness. But this sort of freedom-from does not guarantee our freedom to become creative, responsible and agentive. If we invoke Fromm's classical contribution, we are reminded that our celebrated desire for freedom from all forms of oppression may ultimately be problematic, inasmuch as it may induce a sense of loneliness or of unbearable individual responsibility.[8] Once freed from the bonds of pre-individualistic society – which both provides security and limits our choices – we find that we have not yet gained 'freedom in the positive sense' – that is, the capacity to attain individuation and exercise responsibility. As Fromm reiterates, though freedom-from has brought independence and rationality, it has made us somehow anxious and lonely in our efforts to make choices: 'This isolation is unbearable and the alternatives [the individual] is confronted with are either to escape from the burden of this freedom into new dependencies and submission, or to advance to the full realization of positive freedom which is based upon uniqueness and individuality'[9] – provided we can become sufficiently responsible for the challenges of uniqueness and individuality. In fact, instead of seeking freedom-to, we often seek ways to escape it. But, paradoxically, freedom-to can be equally endangered when attacked through the fight *against* ideologies as it is in the fight *for* any ideologized world view.

Both helplessness and oppression paralyse life, and in order to survive we strive to escape from constraining conditions and gain some cognitive control. But the escape does not restore lost security – however damaging – and may induce us to forget about our own self as a potentially responsible agent. In the language of Fromm, the person 'finds new and fragile security at the expense of sacrificing the integrity of his individual self. He chooses to lose his self since he cannot bear to be alone. This freedom – as freedom-from – leads into new bondage.'[10] Fromm also wonders whether this analysis may lend itself to the well-known belief that there is an inevitable connection between freedom-from and new dependencies. As usual, when confronted with this immemorial problem we come to think that a higher degree of self-awareness may point to the way out of it. It is, in fact, commonly suggested that in psychotherapy a person may achieve a better representation of himself, and thus greater freedom. This suggestion, however, should be carefully qualified, for in fact the ultimate value of a therapeutic process is not primarily the creation of this more realistic representation of the self – which Lear defines as an 'artefact'. In this view, although the subject will become a better observer of himself, the point of treatment is not the appraisal of an accurately represented personality but, rather, the 'unobservational insight into the person creating the representation . . . insight into the forms of active creativity'.[11] In this way, insight into personal, initiatory agency – not into any particular mental representation – can perhaps lead to a renovation of psychic life.

Myths of our culture: Oedipus *and* Orestes

The clinical derivatives of the Oedipus myth seem quite insufficient to explain all the essential maturational advances that we attribute to this famously critical passage. The contention here is that the myth of Orestes could also be fruitfully invoked to illuminate this evolutionary turn. When we are talking of the inner life of human beings, we refer to something that is somehow 'unknown'. The temporal and spatial categories that apply to our tangible world are inadequate, and so we resort to myths and metaphors to help us understand it. Myths and metaphors are our ways of talking about a reality that we cannot directly access. Developmental theories in which we posit particular events happening in infancy could even be regarded as explanatory myths. If we start with reflections on subject and discourse, we can articulate an infinite number of intellectual propositions. If we start instead with stories – myths – of intersubjective vicissitudes, we immediately become involved in specific problems of contingency, responsibility and finitude. Through this route we can probably gain a richer view of our inner conditions.

When an art form like dramatic literature draws upon the myths of a culture for its content, it automatically adopts the basic features and functions of the myth itself. And yet it also becomes a more sophisticated culture fantasy in which the innermost needs and repressed wishes of society can be retraced (and held up in view). This is particularly true of Greek tragedy, for indeed Aeschylus, Sophocles and Euripides all give their individual treatment of some mythological themes without altering the basic structure, outcome or intrinsic content of the myths themselves. In our psychoanalytic culture, the myth of Oedipus has been vastly explored. The myth of Orestes is ultimately ignored. And now, for the sake of clarity, let us recapitulate the two different myths. Disposed of by his royal parents for fear of dethronement, Oedipus survives with adoptive parents, and in the course of time he 'unknowingly' kills his real father and marries his mother – after the ingenious salvation of the city from a persecutory sphinx. The psychological significance of the Oedipus myth implies that the love of the mother remains dominant in the early formative years, and thus inevitably, according to Freud, a perception of the father as a rival becomes insistent for the child to the point that he is drawn into fantasies of destroying this competitor and possessing the mother: the Oedipus 'complex'. In these vicissitudes, the father is experienced as the source of authority that prevents endogamy, and also as capable of punishing the child. The little boy thus abandons his love for the mother and moves on towards identification with the father as the emissary of public language and law – with the consoling understanding that he too may in time occupy such a position of power. The Oedipus complex is for Freud the nucleus of desire, repression and sexual identity. As the complex declines, the superego is formed and becomes part of the topography of the psyche. The struggle to overcome the complex seems never quite resolved. The psychoanalytic encounter may restage the old drama through transference, and the patient is offered a chance to emancipate himself anew.

Turning now to the critical myth of Orestes, we could remark that Freud only dedicates three lines to it: 'The theme . . . is the murder of Agamemnon by his wife Clytemnestra, the vengeance taken on her by their son Orestes, his pursuit by the Furies and his trial and acquittal by the court of the Areopagus in Athens.'[12] And yet, in keeping with his concern for human sexuality, he could have included that Clytemnestra acted in association with her lover Aegisthus; the story says, in fact, that Agamemnon is killed by his spouse *and* by her lover. As a consequence of the vengeance that he enacts, Orestes becomes constantly persecuted by the Furies. The myth also describes a transition from a condition of persecutory thoughts to a more liveable inner world. As is known, the *Oresteia* is a trilogy of plays in which the final one, *The Eumenides*, describes the fate of Orestes after the crime of matricide that incites the Furies, and their subsequent transformation into Eumenides, or consoling creatures. The thesis here is that the myth is essential because not only does it unfold in the endogamous secrecy of the family, but it also involves the community, the admission of responsibility, *and* the experience of acquittal. From a psychoanalytic point of view, there is an essential difference in the inner psychic lives of Oedipus and Orestes. In fact, in neither the Oedipus myth nor in its psychological Freudian rendition is there a mention of the critical value of owning up, admission, acknowledgement. Perhaps some maturational value could be recognized in the little boy's potential for saying/thinking something like this: 'Well, yes, it is me who desires mother.' It is perplexing that the evolutionary value of assuming responsibility for one's attitudes should remain so totally vulnerable to obscurity. Orestes, on the other hand, significantly owns up to his actions when he becomes tried in the assembly of the community. In his capacity as solar deity, Apollo defends Orestes and claims that he must be acquitted because he has assumed responsibility for the crime he has committed. Assuming responsibility for one's own actions and recognizing the authority of the community are perhaps even more seminal and enlightening than the Oedipal vicissitudes of 'simply' identifying with the father. From a psychoanalytic perspective, the Orestes myth implies many more dimensions than the Oedipus paradigm: there is guilt and there is courage, there is family and there is society, there is unbearable psychic pain and there is healing, there is humility and there is affirmative action.

In the *Oresteia* there exists a family situation that has become out of control, and Aeschylus' use of darkness and light as a consistent image depicts a progression from evil to good, from disorder to order. This maturational progress, moreover, seems to require a clear acceptance of responsibility, a measure of remorse, and an interpersonal forgiving background that extends beyond the secrecy of the family. From the beginning of time, vengeance and retribution have been part of the human condition, and this is especially true in Aeschylus' trilogy. In these vicissitudes Orestes suffers a 'mental breakdown', with delusions of the pursuing Furies. And, of course, one does not have to believe that they are real Furies, as distinct from persecutory hallucinations. The system of trial by jury seems indeed created in order to deal with such serious cases and to avoid the vicious cycle of murder and revenge – a cycle comparable to an endless, compulsive chain of reactions. The act of assuming responsibility, of recognizing subjective agency, and the community's attitude of forgiveness appear the key to maturation and development; it is the transformation of a maddening vicious circle into a cumbersome but therapeutic virtuous circle. This makes life difficult for everybody, but it also makes for a richer human life. And thus the evolutionary turning point is not only offered by the Oedipal threatening father, but also by a public space where a rational Apollonian defender may be heard and where a subject may seek ways of emancipation in a climate that in fact presupposes an entirely *new* dimension inspired by the dawning genius of forgiveness. Orestes' assumption of responsibility ultimately transforms the Furies into Eumenides. Forgiveness is not at all easy, but it is not impossible. And if forgiveness is difficult to grant and to receive, it is equally difficult to conceptualize. In the seminal myth of Orestes, the psychic scenario of forgiveness is revealed. The individual appears at last as an agentive subject who accepts being bound to his action.

Chapter 9

Empathy and sympathy

Preliminaries

As is known, authors often use the terms 'empathy' and 'sympathy' interchangeably. The term 'sympathy' is often used when the term 'empathy' would be more accurate – and vice versa. As contrasted with 'sympathy', which has a 'longer history' (and, in fact, is also used by Darwin), 'empathy' is a modern word, probably coined as a translation of the German *Einfühlung*.

Whatever the appropriate, conventional significance of these words, we should remark that the phenomena describable in terms of either 'sympathy' or 'empathy' can be quite different and diversified. Some are more complex, challenging and creative; some are more 'mechanical', repetitive and foreseeable. Some are more narcissistically sustained, while others are more object-oriented. In light of the more elaborate, complex and challenging features commonly attributed to the experience of empathy, one may be inclined to regard it as the more mature of the two attitudes. More recently, empathy has come to be regarded as involving not only some recognition and understanding of another's emotional state (however minimal), but also the complexive experience of the other person's actual or inferred emotional state.[1] We often use the terms 'empathy' and/or 'sympathy' simply for lack of a better term, and thus we sometimes overextend or unduly restrict their respective meanings. Within the domain of the humanities, we primarily use our limited natural languages and thus have to constantly contextualize, adapt and qualify our terms. Frequently overlapping in use, the respective meanings of 'sympathy' and 'empathy' are thus also determined by the context in which they are inserted. Having no claim to establish lexical stipulations, we only try to juxtapose 'sympathy' and 'empathy' in order to argue that the latter may serve to indicate the more mature, initiatory and intentional attitudes – indeed, the attitudes that sustain human spontaneity. We should also remark that, according to Black, 'Sympathy . . . makes empathy possible, but they operate at different levels of sophistication; *empathy* is a sophisticated and conscious act, which uses as a tool the elementary and inescapable (involuntary) capacity that . . . Hume would call *sympathy*.'[2] Perhaps he regards sympathy as a developmental precursor of empathy, just as Gaddini differentiates between imitation and internalization, in the sense that imitation is an inchoate phase of internalization proper.[3] For the sake of simplicity, we could begin by consulting the *Pocket Oxford Dictionary* and see that 'sympathy' is defined as 'Being simultaneously affected with the same feeling as another; capacity for this; sharing . . . in emotion, or sensation or condition; compassion or approval (for); agreement in opinion or desire.' 'Empathy', however, is presented as indicating the 'Power' – no less than power! – 'of identifying oneself mentally with (and so *fully comprehending*) a person or object of contemplation.'[4] But then, without 'fully comprehending' another, how could we honestly say that – in sympathy – we can be 'affected with the *same* feeling as another' or that we can share in emotion, sensation, condition? Or how could we honestly experience compassion and express approval? No less a thinker than Kierkegaard refers to inadequate ways of empathizing as the 'silly participation in others, which is falsely honoured by the name of sympathy, whereas it is in fact nothing but vanity'.[5]

With this same outlook, we could also appreciate an enlightening paradox: if we invoke a passage by the philosopher Hume, we see him using the term 'sympathy' as if he were instead referring to the different and more challenging attitude of 'empathy'. He says: 'No quality of human nature is more remarkable . . . than the propensity we have to sympathize with others, and to receive by communication their inclinations and sentiments.'[6] And, of course, anyone would agree with such a remark; but the problem is that he concludes this same sentence with an apparently minor qualification: 'however different from or contrary to our own'. But then, the point is that we simply cannot manage to experience sympathy when 'inclinations and sentiments are different from or contrary to our own'. We can only sympathize with those with whom we are prepared, conditioned or induced to sympathize by nature or by culture, so to speak. In fact, we simply do not sympathize with views or attitudes that are different or even contrary to our own. Hume further says: 'To this principle [sympathy] we ought to ascribe the great uniformity we may observe in the humours and turn of thinking of those of the *same* nation.' But then, the philosopher here clearly implies that we could hardly have any sympathy for those of a *different* nation – whatever a nation is. And he finally concludes: 'So remarkable a phenomenon merits our attention, and must be trac'd up to its first principles.'[7] The 'first principles' perhaps refer to the comparative prevalence of either narcissism or object-relatedness in the human attitudes that we seek to understand.

Although Freud does not explicitly theorize a distinction, in his work the 'clinician' definitely captures the difference between sympathy and empathy: 'We are far from having exhausted the problem of identification, and we are faced by the process which psychology calls "empathy" [*Einfühlung*], and which plays the largest part in our understanding of what is inherently *foreign* to our ego in other people.'[8] The adjective 'foreign' is especially significant. Indeed, it is a word that commonly indicates those of a *different* nation – almost as if it were a commentary on Hume's 'humours and turns of thinking' of those of the *same* nation, those with whom we can 'naturally' sympathize. Sympathy only functions with those with whom we are inclined – or perhaps compelled, driven, forced – to sympathize, as, for instance, one's favourite nephew, selfobject (in the analytic jargon), or fellow devotee within any ideological group. And *all* of our sympathies are customarily re-styled in glorified terms for which we also produce an appropriate rhetoric. In psychopathological terms, moreover, we could say that most perversions, however destructive, seem rooted in some form of phantasmal sympathy. And thus we use this reading of 'sympathy' in order to contrast it more clearly with the cognate but psychologically stronger significance of 'empathy'. Sympathy can be expected as a natural mechanism, while empathy is largely unpredictable and also tends to expand our relational field in a creative way. We tend to separate good and bad objects by means of our sympathy, but we can identify new features, new difference-bearing characteristics, or unseen 'gifts' by means of our empathic capacities. And this is the manifestation of spontaneity: one is simply drawn *into* sympathetic connections, whereas one does creatively strive *towards* empathic contacts. In the words of Black, empathy 'is a sophisticated act of the imagination, a "trial identification" done by someone who is consciously relating to another's mental state'.[9]

For the intelligent, symbolic creatures that we are, those for whom we have no sympathy or even antipathy, and with whom we cannot develop empathy, must be somehow proven wrong, and ultimately abjected. And yet, although we may succeed in defeating our 'adversaries' by proving them wrong, they often do not change their convictions or abandon their concerns. This might be an indication that they pursue an ulterior goal or form of knowledge that is not captured by our reversed sympathy, or antipathy. There may be a great deal of residual, essential rationality that is not appreciated when we turn away from antagonists, and which is thus left out of our stringent adversarial tests. Proving others wrong may be as cogent an enterprise as it is ultimately futile; by combating another's detestable conviction, we may persistently miss the point that is determining the conviction, which is an empathic failure.[10] Empathy is often totally marginalized in the deployment of sympathy, which often seems compulsory, whereas empathy is largely initiatory, intentional, spontaneous; in the attitude of empathy we are not determined by external factors, but we tend to act of our own accord. But what is this accord? It is possibly a condition deriving from a sufficient level of accord among inner parts, from being sufficiently integrated, coordinated and thus psychically alive, not deadened by pervasive splitting; and the more we incline to a condition of inner deadness, the more we become restricted to relations of sympathy – as contrasted with the challenges of empathy.

In the classical contribution entitled *On the Problem of Empathy*, Stein brilliantly explores this essential human capacity, which, in fact, should be appreciated as a *problem* rather than a merely 'natural' psychic mechanism. 'Sympathized and empathized joy' – she says – 'need not necessarily be the same in content at all. They are certainly not the same in respect to quality, since one is a primordial and the other is a non-primordial experience.'[11] Although for Stein 'primordial' does not mean 'primitive' or 'inchoate', empathy for her clearly indicates a complex, developed and comprehensive inner phenomenon. Conversely, when she (rarely) introduces the term 'sympathy', she significantly remarks that 'We can designate this primordial act as . . . fellow-feeling [sympathy]'[12] – as in the case of those of the 'same nation'. But then, an intriguing and perplexing adjective such as 'foreign' also surfaces in Stein's work. With her inimitable acumen she seems to suggest that when there is a condition of being submerged by the other, and a condition of oneness rather than a state of relation with a 'foreign' object, what appears to be empathy becomes reduced to sympathy. In her language: 'In all cases there is a distinction between the transference of feeling and, not only empathy, but also sympathy and a feeling of oneness, these latter being based on an empathic *submersion* in the foreign experience.'[13] Empathy is not a fusional feeling of submersion, she insists. She adds: 'Not through the feeling of oneness, but through empathising, do we experience others. . . . The enrichment of our experience becomes possible through empathy'[14] – and certainly not through any form of fusional submersion.

Narcissism and sympathy

Symington reiteratively suggests that it is the 'turning away from' the others that forms the core of narcissism. And this is not to be found in one part or in another, but in the way in which the self relates to others, or even to its inner objects.[15] And thus narcissism could be envisaged in terms of a generalized resulting attitude, a style or principle that strictly limits the acceptability of psychic experiences. And even when on the surface there is no narcissism, deep in one's heart one may have nothing to do with the other and may thus opt for circumscribed sympathies rather than expanding empathies.

Frailty and vulnerability are arguably universal problems, but that does not mean that everyone should necessarily empathize with this very human condition. For that to happen, human beings would perhaps need to develop a sense of empathy with the same passionate commitment that earlier generations experienced when they substituted democracy for different forms of totalitarianism. But then, empathy is not easy to develop and practise. Creative empathy, for instance, requires a capacity to perspectivally visualize whatever relations we may be involved with – at the extreme, even relations between those that inflict wounds and our wounded selves. This capacity would enable us to capture the miserly condition of one who can only inflict injury and produce poisonous 'nourishment'. For clarity's sake, we could extrapolate Black's dramatic analogy and say that professional torturers tormenting their victims must be very 'sympathetic' to their victims. In another sense, of course, they are horribly unsympathetic. They somehow 'know' what it must feel like, but they sadly know without compassion, without empathy.[16]

Developing human beings are linked to outer figures for reasons of survival and cannot entirely forswear their caretakers – although they can, of course, hate them. Development may also sometimes turn inwards to inner figures that are extremely good or bad, *and* unreal. Every effort is then made to make outer figures conform to those inner imagos, and they are opportunely manipulated into this conformity.[17] Paradoxically, when people are seen as persecutory, they may turn out to be in sympathetic accord with our view of the world – and we may even revolt when they prove to be neutral or benevolent. The rationale of this hatred is that we resent the existence of an autonomous other, and in order to sustain the illusion that others are not entitled to exist as they are, every effort is made to seduce them into our sympathy and to ensure that they do not become legitimate others – that is, independent subjects. And thus it is the potential impact on the self by the other that is fiercely resented; this impact must be strictly controlled. Feelings can, in fact, function in two different ways. If we are under the dominance of narcissistic currents, our feelings all tend to register how things affect our feelings, and we thus only select objects with whom we can enact our subjective sympathy in either a manipulated or phantasmal way. But feelings can operate in a different way when they reach out and capture difference-bearing features of the subject with whom we interact.

In most theoretical models, narcissism is said to occur when the ego takes itself as an erotic object or, to put it in classical Freudian terminology, when the libido takes its own self as a love-object. And yet, it is not only this celebrated, mysterious 'self' that we turn to but also – or especially – selfobjects. These are the narcissistically used persons whom we constantly seek to introject: those who only exist because they are turned into our selected, imploded objects. There is perhaps nothing more intoxicating than self-love. Silverman remarks that on those rare occasions when we imaginarily coincide with the ideal imago that we worship languishingly from afar, we live through absolute thrilling experiences. Indeed, one could go as far as suggesting that the pleasures afforded by even the most intense object-love are eclipsed by those provided by a narcissistic involvement. At such rapturous moments, however, the subject is filled up in a dangerous way.

However imaginary, this abundance is contrary to the operations of desire and, therefore, to human existence in its manifold dimensions.[18] As long as it continues, there is in effect no spontaneity, no other and no world.

The refusal of otherness should be carefully explored if we keep in mind that the narcissistic attitude is a basic pattern underlying all the different psychopathologic conditions, or mental illnesses. The narcissist uses the object not in sharing interdependency, but for a disguised parasitic relationship in which the object has to be reduced and controlled, so as to remain omnipotent and 'sympathetic'. The narcissist may hate object relations, but he is stuck with them and so has to manipulate others to his pathological needs in the most sentimental and decorative way.[19] Narcissists hate needing their objects, but they deny their feelings of envy by extracting in fantasy those aspects of the object that they need, so as to bypass the intense struggle of envy and gratitude. There are no such prosaic negotiations – just glorified sympathy. The idea that sympathy is a rather rudimentary psychic attitude and more closely propelled by our instinctual condition could perhaps be connected to the popular current discussions about 'mirror neurons'. In fact, sympathy may be a propensity that directly derives from the soma in terms of neurological mirroring, which works by automatically initiating the mimicry of a perceived affective display. From the perspective of Matte Blanco's bi-logic,[20] sympathy is, of course, closer to the symmetrical, mirroring relations – as distinct from the asymmetrical ones.

In the early phases of development, sympathy may function by highlighting particular features while others are eclipsed, including ones that are of the highest survival relevance for the individual with whom we try to relate. We can readily think of certain adult metaphors that afflict our young: they not only obscure specific capacities, but actually cause them to atrophy by consistently ignoring their function. The ultimate danger is a pre-emptive psychic damage that actually prevents the development of a potential; it is a loss that cannot even be decried by the individual because there is no way of arguing that a certain 'unknown' quality has been excluded from development. Thus, empathy may enhance the growth of spontaneity in one's own self and in the others, while sympathy alone ultimately hinders it. Whenever inchoate or later aspects of inner life do not encounter sufficient empathy, it is like being told that we should relinquish or ignore them. These circumstances may drive a developing individual to retreat from full personhood by allowing the extinction of vital parts of the mind. But empathy can, of course, be sought from alternative, second-best sources. Under these circumstances of disadvantage, it takes genius to attempt metaphoric connections attributing the name of one thing, on which we have an affectual grasp, to another thing that we tentatively would like to catch, identify or invest.

Benjamin appropriately specifies that in the dialectics between recognition and negation, it is essential to render the negating aspect conspicuous, for it is in fact an attempt to negate the difference and otherness of the other. This negating moment is crucial in the problem of accepting difference and otherness.[21] The different other is a threat to the identity of the self (or ego) that wants both to be all there is and to assimilate everything into itself in an atmosphere of total, seamless sympathy. Benjamin aims to show how the intersubjective relation can even keep alive the negating moment while maintaining the possibility of recognition; it is indeed a problematic coexistence of attitudes. With this outlook, we can perceive 'control' as the absolute precondition for possessing the other, for it is hardly thinkable that one may succeed in ingesting – or homogenizing, or capturing – someone who is intent on actively expressing his own unicity. In certain 'treatments', the patient manages to sympathetically ingest the therapist's way of seeing things into the surface of the personality, while the inner affective core is in fact hostile and eager to control the other's creative thinking. And yet, below the level of consciousness, or perhaps even consciously, the patient may feel 'bad', with an ultimate stifling effect on his potential for spontaneity. Those who cannot be spontaneous may constantly try to seduce others to give them encouragement; they may even make a great display of concerned sympathy while being completely indifferent and constantly trying to conceal their narcissistic strategy. By not opting for a relation to otherness, they pre-emptively impede their source of action and intentionality. Why? Because nothing needs to be done or even attempted if we find everything inside. No agency, creativity or intentionality is allowed; there is nothing to be negotiated and no reciprocal adjustments are needed. In the long run, refined manipulation is opted for and no aspiration to spontaneity survives. No amount of gratification is ever sufficient as a remedy for inner changelessness.

Low-cost sympathy

When inner conditions prevail that are only hospitable to emotions comparable to our own, we are strongly inclined to selectively sympathize as if it were a 'spontaneous' reaction, or a natural psychic response; thus, we share something only to the extent that it is also our own. At the extreme, sympathy seems to be both a narcissistic and a mechanical response. When we consider the naturalness and easiness of sympathy and our own propensity for it, we should also realize that this inclination – somewhat like a psychic force of gravity – is primarily induced by mechanisms of identification with selfobjects rather than with autonomous selves. It is psychically natural for us to sympathize with those who are generically *like* us, to cheer for one's 'secret' team, or to stand for one's nation – at no *psychic* cost, whatever the *tangible* costs. As is known, even fierce tyrants or mafia bosses can be sentimental and sympathetic to their devout spouses or domestic animals; they are even ready to suffer for and with them. It is therefore essential that the cost-free naturalness of sympathy should be kept quite distinct from the laborious spontaneity of empathy. We should thus appreciate a contrast with regard to attitudes that are natural but not spontaneous. Natural sympathy involves no psychic labour or cost. Spontaneous empathy comes at the price of maturational struggles. At the core of narcissism there is perhaps a hatred of the psychic *cost* of relating – a hatred of something that is inherent to our own being. A relationship implies two or more partners; if the two sympathetically converge into the same entity, there can no longer be a relationship between the two. In its hatred of the relational, one of the ways in which narcissism operates is the implacable erosion of separateness in thought and feeling.

Sympathy only seems to allow connections supported by narcissistic currents through which we regard others as if they were parts of our own self. Whenever the interlocutor who putatively has greater responsibility within a bi-personal field is not sufficiently aware of how challenging it is to make contact with the depths of his own self in order to attempt empathic – as contrasted with merely sympathetic – contacts, the relationship will be steered towards his own standards of inner life; in this way, the costly risk of attempting unexpected, disquieting connections can be avoided. The more 'responsible' one in the dyad might only take the pathways that are already well known and that present no threat to the narcissistic epistemology that he inhabits. However unnoticed and appropriate, this attitude amounts to an irresponsible way of dealing with the other's creative potential. Even in analysis the therapist may succumb to the transference role of a like-minded, narcissistic object; but being drawn into this role is, of course, the analyst's problem.[22] In fact, underestimation of these difficulties of transference vicissitudes may easily induce the analyst to achieve empathic contact 'by force', so to speak, turning the enterprise into a stereotyped task.[23] The parody of this therapeutic posture may silently draw the patient into a condition of conscious gratitude and unconscious resentment. When we are under the dominance of narcissistic currents, then we are just feeling the way in which we are affected, and this further precludes our attitude of contact with the other. We refuse the cost of this attitude. The 'relation' thus involves minimal areas of the other's personality, and we create the delusion of convergence and homogenization. 'We have the same feelings and share the same values' – so the story goes.

The person that the narcissist tries to include into his own self may, of course, attempt to survive. And the decision to survive destruction by homogenization is a *spontaneous* act, an action proper, and an intentional attitude. In whichever context or maturational phase, the decision enhances sanity for all those involved. Any minimal attempt in this direction is capable of breaking the most vicious of circles. Even if by all appearances nothing actually changes, the intention to survive reduces the damage to a mere incursion on the part of the attacker, rather than to a symbiotic collusion. And, paradoxically, defeating the attacker by means of a decision to survive is the greatest psychic gift that the attacker might receive: whenever the narcissist meets with the other's refusal to coincide in a fusional manner, he may begin to think of himself as a separate being and as not irremediably destructive – bad. In order *not* to be destroyed, one strives to be spontaneous, to act *sua sponte*, of his own inner accord – and willing to live on for his own sake. This is the converse of lapsing into constrained sympathy with narcissistic seductions.

In transitional experiencing, the infant's sense of freedom is linked to a limitless feeling of wholeness, prior to raising the question of absolute limits. According to Eigen, the new awakening in object usage involves the realization that the other is in some basic way outside one's boundaries, that he is wholly other.[24] And while this may precipitate some transient disorganization, it culminates in enhancing the subject's sense of aliveness. It is like being born for the second time, into a different sort of psychic breathing in which a genuine 'not-me' nutrient becomes available for one's personal metabolism. Through the risks of difference as such, we gain access to the genuinely new.

Denying the other's potential and privileging the sympathetic choices of the authorial authority of those who do the talking, and have the last word, can be seriously detrimental for the young ones. For instance, denying the inner life of a little boy who is terrified (because we cannot empathize with his terror) and addressing him with metaphoric clichés such as 'But you are my little, brave lion!', or else stifling the anger of a little girl (because we cannot accept it) with comparable utterances such as 'But you are my little angel!', are common ways of using pseudo-empathic attitudes to stifle psychic life. Those metaphors that are successfully absorbed into the literality of any phatic community become powerful instruments for appreciating something and ignoring something else. If, for instance, 'Richard is a lion' and 'John is a mouse' become literal in the comparatively short life cycle of a family language, then such 'hard facts' as Richard's courage and John's fearfulness become totally natural, like the 'obvious' realities incorporated into the literal linguisticity of any group. And they are so powerful that Richard, against his own nature, may be compelled to act brave to the point of damaging himself, while John may restrain his natural combative potential and similarly deteriorate his inner life. Thus, in order to develop one's spontaneity, we may have to migrate in search of novel linguistic communities that may allow for new styles of psychic survival and creative action.[25]

In this connection it may be appropriate to invoke Bion's reflection on the psychoanalyst's effort to understand the vicissitudes of the relation with the analysand. In his view, formulations can be judged by considering how necessary the existence of the analyst is to the thoughts that he expresses:

'The more his interpretations can be judged as showing how necessary *his* knowledge, *his* experience, *his* character are to the thought as formulated, the more reason there is to suppose that the interpretation is psychoanalytically worthless.'[26] Is it simply worthless, or is it actually detrimental? Such interpretations, in fact, may be focusing on the analyst's own way of doing things and not on what the patient is trying to convey on the basis of a negotiated agreement. This sort of interpretation can feel especially sympathetic because it profoundly resonates with the 'natural' personality of the analyst; it is a natural expression inasmuch as he feels drawn to a certain way of seeing things. And this is the only possible way, simply because it is his usual way. The analyst's potential for being innovative and insightful is ultimately not used. Also, this potential may be weakened by restricting it within the scope of sympathy and by inclining towards endogamic, narcissistic, claustrophilic ventures.

With differing degrees of complexity, human beings seem to develop a complexive view of reality at their earliest opportunity; through this, they supplement what they know nothing about with derivatives of that same complexive view of themselves in the world. When confronted with surprising situations, we are tempted to produce accounts of the new experience in terms of our own innermost picture of things – our only currency – and thus we incorporate new experiences on our own terms and do not face renovation costs. Connections can thus be arresting: that copular 'is' that could be described as creating connection may easily involve an abuse that entraps the interlocutor. Metaphoric connections thus both open and foreclose. In any macro- or micro-community (even a dyad) in which the sympathetic expressions of the emblematic adult seem to thrive – and tend to become dominant – certain restrictive and distorting mental attitudes are reinforced, possibly degrading the quality of psychic life in the phatic community.

While sympathy is a natural inclination, empathy is a creative venture. Sympathy is the capacity for very short moves that may not exceed our narcissistic sphere, while empathy is a capacity for a more extensive move that reaches the difference-bearing features of the other. Whenever the exploration of one's inner world is consistently taken over and articulated by others, the sort of insight for coping with vicissitudes of hope and despair, of attachments and separations, may not properly develop. Such a surrender of one's profound experiences to the sympathy of the superior managers of language and culture could be seen as encouraging the atrophy of one's inner life. The authoritative, articulate other may sympathize with those features that are not at all essential or critical to one's inner life. Through the uncritical use of sympathy by the adult, and a limited capacity for empathy in the developing person, contacts can be transformed into violence. Quite a deadening atmosphere comes to prevail. Indeed, the territorial and predatory heritage of hominization is thus transferred from the biological to the dialogical level and enacted in the symbolic domain through the apparently neutral attitudes that sustain sympathy; in fact, as a species, we now have to cope more with the challenges of culture than with the dangers of nature.

Scheler reports a story drawn from the work of Schopenhauer as an allegory of a problematic style in the identificatory process. The fable induces the reader to think of identification in corporeal terms and thus, somehow, in terms of a bodily ego. 'A white squirrel, having met the gaze of a snake, hanging on a tree and showing every sign of a mighty appetite for its prey, is so terrified by this that it gradually moves towards instead of away from the snake, and finally throws itself into the open jaws. . . . Plainly the squirrel's instinct for self-preservation has succumbed to an *ecstatic participation* in the object of the snake's own appetitive nisus, namely "swallowing". The squirrel identifies in feeling with the snake, and thereupon spontaneously establishes corporeal identity with it, by disappearing down in its throat.'[27] This sort of identification, says Scheler, effects 'the total eclipse and absorption of another self by one's own, it being thus, as it were, completely dispossessed and deprived of all rights in its conscious existence and character.'

Empathy and otherness

Empathy thus seems to involve diverse factors such as cognitive, inferential and synthetic capacities; it is, in fact, relatively neutral and non-judgemental, unlike the related phenomena of pity and sympathy – from which it should be distinguished. According to Moore and Fine, sympathy lacks objectivity, encourages overidentification and sometimes leads to the enactment of rescue fantasies.[28] As contrasted with the 'naturalness' of sympathy, empathy can be the end result of a truly laborious process; as a consequence, a caricature of empathy may sometimes prevail that is ultimately a parody of the life-enhancing function of empathy. The pervasive effects of this parodic attitude may even induce one to stereotypically 'empathize', as if compelled by the latest fashion. But then, at the receiving end, creatures often seem to spontaneously curtail and restrict these expressions within narrow inner spaces because of the fear of being homogenized, converted or absorbed by the unrequested pseudo-empathy of 'authoritative' figures.

As a parallel to this prospect, or as a contrast to it, the critical attitude that inclines us to mental health, or pathology, seems to be a matter of choice, decision or acceptance – however minimally conscious or inchoative. It is the choice to accept a gift coming from something or somewhere outside oneself – as contrasted with refusing it. It is the decision to hold on to a challenging gift, however paradoxical or 'strange' that gift may be. It is the acceptance of the basic otherness that we accept to deal with for the sake of a realistic approach to life. This hypothesis can be clinically fertile inasmuch as through it we can better observe the splits, denials and never-ending detours that are necessary for survival whenever the basic sense of otherness has been ignored and refused. The differing other comes into being through being chosen, a little like the way gestaltic patterns come into being through our creative perceptual action. The option makes the differing other acceptable; the paradox here is that it has independent existence, yet it does not exist for us without being opted for.

Bearing in mind that 'empathy' and 'sympathy' are often used inter-changeably, we could once again invoke Freud; referring to the *starec* Zosima of *The Brothers Karamazov*, he says: 'The holy man is rejecting the temptation to despise or detest the murderer and for that reason humbles himself before him. Dostoevsky's sympathy for the criminal is in fact boundless; it goes far beyond the pity which the unhappy wretch has a right to, and reminds us of the "holy awe" with which epileptics and lunatics were regarded in the past.'[29] In fact, going beyond pity is a move towards empathy; and when sympathy is 'boundless', that means that it has not been coerced by narcissistic currents of sympathy. Whenever the inhabitation of our world view is not sufficiently recognized, it may endanger our spon-taneity inasmuch as curiosity is virtually rendered useless – and thus we have no space for the differing other. Epistemophily in fact manifests itself through a passion for radical listening, for discovery, so that one may understand *and* accept, perceive limits *and* make connections, allow con-frontation *and* recognize difference;[30] the force of human epistemophily is evidenced in metaphoric efforts to generate 'impossible' questions and con-nections – in the way in which the *starec* Zosima relates with the 'unhappy wretch'. In standing up to otherness, one can appreciate its distinguishing character and innovative potential. This spontaneous accepting attitude leaves others in that 'elsewhere' that bears them, leaving their strangeness intact. This implies a resistance to the 'natural' inclination to control others for the sake of domestication and conversion. Empathy aims to make contacts and to cope with that differing something, without representing its structure according to our own inner idols or trying to reshape it. If victimized by our inner idolatry, a hierarchy must necessarily be established whereby we become entitled to convert others. Hierarchy and homogeniza-tion are indivisible as hierarchy is always grounded on the assumption that differences are only differences of degree on a putative commensurable scale. What needs to be emphasized is that in the act of acceptance, it is the act itself that structures empathy. And conversely, the attitude of empathy supports the process of acceptance. When the inner action is one of both empathy and acceptance, 'we call our perceptions real and our beliefs sane'.[31]

The problem of how we relate to the fact that the other's consciousness is independent – that his mind is fundamentally like our own, but unfathomably different and outside our control – has been a line running through psychoanalytic thinking. Our celebrated 'objects' are in fact legitimate, free, agentive subjects. The essence of the recognition of otherness could perhaps be simplified in a Freud-like language by suggesting that 'Where objects were, there subjects should be.' According to Benjamin, central to this task is the matter of how we use our marvellous capacity for identification with others to either further or impede our recognition of others, to bridge or obfuscate differences between us; or, rather, we could be concerned with how we do both at once.[32] This whole problem leads to a concern for the radical effects of perspective – that is, the necessity of struggling to grasp the viewpoint of another as well as to strain our viewpoint through the critical filter of analysis. Easily said, but not so easily done. Benjamin suggests that omnipotence is always a central problem for the self, disavowed rather than worked through by its position as rational subject. 'In fact, if the other were not a problem for the subject, the subject would again be absolute – either absolutely separate or assimilating the other. Therefore, the negativity that the other sets up for the self has its own possibilities, a productive irritation, heretofore insufficiently explored.'[33] Seeking to grasp the real process involved in attaining an approximation of another's viewpoint (or even glimpses of it) is central to our distinction between empathy and sympathy and also to 're-evaluate–re-appraise' the function of otherness.[34]

Empathy implies a willingness not to react from personality but, rather, to act in the sense of opening up to something that is beyond our personality and that can then inform our action and prompt it.[35] It functions like the reception of some 'strange' gift from the real *other*, which can only occur in a situation that is beyond our limited personality and in which we dare to open up boundaries for a transformative contact – not in a situation in which we merely react. These essential, transformational experiences could be expressed in Eigen's language: he speaks of 'floating freely in a joyous shock of difference. At this moment one is enlivened and quickened through the sense of difference. One is sustained sheerly through the unfolding sense of self–other presencing, a presencing no longer taken for granted but appreciated as coming through . . . turning into joyous appreciation of one another's mystery. The real here is self and other feeling real to one another, breaking past residues of depersonalization–derealization.'[36] The quality of these experiences, however, is not comparable to fusional states; to express this critical difference in Weil's essential language, we could in fact say that 'To love is to consent to distance, it is to adore the distance between ourselves and that which we love.'[37]

We could say that the way any two, or more, interlocutors know that they have entered real empathy, and that it is distinct from the more usual exchanges of sympathy, is that these experiences, paradoxically, may even appear unfamiliar, unexpected in their specific form and timing, or 'strange'; it may even be confusing as to what is happening or what should be done. And yet the contact becomes very intense subjectively, as in the more transformational moments of truth. As suggested by Bollas, there are experiences that we know of although we cannot quite think of them.[38] And, of course, whatever is known but not sufficiently thought cannot be properly expressed, but only very indirectly communicated, perhaps also in order to mitigate its alien or innovative quality. Therefore, no communication will take place on the basis of our quasi-mechanical subjective sympathy; what is required is a sufficiently developed attitude of empathy for getting in touch with whatever in the other may be suspected of being known but not yet thought – however strange, foreign or incongruous.

In life-enhancing interactions, the early expressions of the nascent personality are met with construals creating the belief that language is an enriching instrument and a path to community formation. But in those pseudo-construals whereby psychic life tends to become sadly detached from linguistic life, there is no interpretative response to the inventive attempts of the evolving individual; there is, instead, a tendency to direct the exchange towards the literalness of the adult's language or to whatever vocabulary is dominant. A centrifugal sort of language, leading away from the core of the self, is firmly established, and through it we come to believe that real life and ordinary language are to be ultimately dissociated inasmuch as one's own language is to be regarded as inessential to projects of survival and coexistence. This centrifugal force seems contrary to any empathic contact; it is the inconspicuous (and thus unquestioned) equivalent of intimating that there is no logic whatsoever in *the other*'s abjected mind, that real logic is only to be found in the emissary of the dominant world view, and that one must seek access to it if there is an aspiration to be something more than a merely natural living being. By a constant deviation from what is personal to what is conventional, one may become deprived of instruments for self-reflection and, in turn, for appreciating the inner life of still others.

The realistic and phantasmal representations of our others are not necessarily in conflict and may interact in a mutually enriching way. These two psychic realities, on the other hand, can be played against each other by the non-empathic member of any dyad, and a destructive crossing may take place. One may try to play, while the other may respond as if it were a serious attack and thus threaten retaliation in return. Or one of the two may be terribly serious about a specific distress, while the other responds as if it were an occasion for playing. In both cases there is no creative playing, no interaction or empathy, but only a mechanical reaction or acting out. Play is, of course, nullified if others take it 'seriously' – that is, if they take it seriously in the wrong way; for instance, in not understanding the playful quality of the move and then responding with mad seriousness, 'You want to attack me and thus I threaten you.' This may escalate into a perverse way of relating, in the sense that if no contact can be gained through play, it may still be obtained through violence.

The future of empathy

We often read that the goal of much twentieth-century feminist thinking was to resist the role of being the feminine 'other' to the masculine 'I', by means of rethinking difference and otherness. The question, basically, was how could women differentiate themselves and their otherness from the identity-as-other imposed on them by the male-dominated traditions from which they perceived themselves to be alienated because of their gender. But then, persons can probably be alienated on account of ethnicity or of any other characteristics. And thus this same clarifying attitude and revolt against alienation could be creatively at work in a variety of different situations in which our genius for empathy can be developed and exercised. In other words, anyone can fully exist, even apart from the identity-as-other imposed by any dominant interlocutor. And, more importantly, we can constantly try to safeguard the other's otherness in the most disparate conditions. One of the central questions is how we might respond to having our assumptions questioned from the perspectives of others who do not associate themselves with the traditions within which we operate. The hermeneutical condition out of which this question arises is, of course, global and transnational. In a psychic and cultural atmosphere in which the inclinations of sympathy prevail upon the creative challenges of empathy, the end result may be a 'creative' propensity to primarily challenge the tradition from within and to resent challenges emanating from outer, 'alien' sources – who should not exist as epistemic subjects, or as creatures who can return our critical gaze. It is dubious whether there can be a real understanding of our objects of knowledge that preserves and recognizes the otherness of the other. In Code's view, it is perhaps more accurate to read tradition as the history of the winners, which gains authority because the memory of the dissenters, or the silenced, is forgotten – and thus truth largely becomes another name for success.[39]

In the modern age, reason became the coveted behaviour for securing progress. In the new era, reason-included-into-empathy is perhaps the human resource to cope with our shared vulnerability as well as the key to global awareness. To empathize is to cross over and experience, in the most profound way, the very being of another – especially the other's struggle to endure and prevail in his life journey. Empathy is the ultimate expression of communication between creatures. It is virtually the 'real thing', as contrasted with the display of innumerable pretences; it is our most precious resource, and always scarce. In our 'global village' we should perhaps revive the pristine meaning of *economy*, which etymologically means 'home science': *oicos* (home) and *nomos* (rule), indicating a zeal for the best way to manage a home, with no waste, and survival for all. But then, those with whom we cannot sympathize become, automatically, adversarial figures to be expelled from a home – figures on which we project unbearable affects and which are worthy only of an exclusionary gaze. If the actual costs of sympathy could be calculated in terms of tangible resources – and in our computational culture of simulations this is a possibility – we would perhaps appreciate their 'unthinkable' magnitude in economic terms. Most of us could easily indulge in the fantasy of what it would be like if groups and nations were relatively free of paranoid preoccupations, not so imprisoned in their sympathies and more capable of empathy; the fantasy could easily develop into a transfer of resources from the ministries of 'defence' – a significant coincidence of terms – onto the ministries of agriculture or even just culture – another interesting linguistic coincidence. In the long sweep of human history, what is becoming clear is that the human journey is, at its core, about the extension of empathy to broader and more inclusive domains. Empathy is something that reveals itself to us if we are open to the experience – and we are more often open when we have experienced personal hardship and travails in our own individual journeys towards enduring the burden of life, and towards development. While the human journey is often made slower by defeats and failures of great magnitude, our saving grace is that the hardships we endure, both individually and collectively, can prepare us to be open to the plight of different others and to champion their causes.[40]

In so-called postmodern literature, the topic of empathy is experiencing an inflationary success, and empathy comes to appear as potentially capable of profoundly influencing the course of interactive events. Yet empathy should be attentively considered if we are not to create a myth of it, and if we want to look for its stronger character both as a goal and as a method. For the sake of exploring its stronger meaning, we could pro- visionally say that our more natural sympathy could be a weaker and less mature version of empathy. If empathy were simply a natural attitude somehow comparable to sympathy – that is, the manifestation of the psycho-biological qualities of certain individuals – then it would be impossible to see it as the lengthy, laborious maturational achievement that it often is. In her elaborate *Reflections on Gender and Science*, Keller remarks that as the result of long travail, 'both sense of self and of other become sufficiently secure to permit momentary relaxation of the boundary between the two – without, that is, threatening the loss of either'.[41] From, a generic cognitive perspective, we could also agree with Bordo, who draws on Keller and insists that a renovated foundation of knowledge is rooted not in detachment but in connectedness and empathy.[42] Paradoxically, we might have to develop a sense of empathy towards our own self, our paradoxical otherness – what sometimes goes by the name of 'capacity of insight', in psychoanalytic jargon. By way of example, Silverman remarks that contact with the homeless poor or with the very ill makes it difficult to identify with their structural position; proximity and encounter make it difficult to imagine that in such a situation we would still coincide with that 'psychological fiction' that we call 'we'. There are experiences that dispel this fiction by indicating that, for instance, if we became very ill or very poor we would no longer coincide with ourselves.[43] And rather than acceding to this imperative self-estrangement, we frequently avert our psychic gaze.

Empathy and community

Human beings exhibit the capacity not only to make use of what is culturally canonical (even if only referring to a dyadic micro-community), but also to identify deviations that potentially constitute the source of new stories, accounts or contacts. Such deviations become conspicuous by means of initiatory connections through which we can attempt further interpretations of our individual insight into strangeness and unfamiliarity. One of our precious human talents is the capacity to renegotiate affects and significance by means of empathic connections that often take the form of a narrative. Creativeness involves an ability both to appreciate the principles of normality and to accurately account for deviations. Creativity surpasses existing syntheses in such a way that new questions come to have sense. But then, how do we find a new element to *hook* if we do not have the empathic force to invest it ('cathect it', in the jargon) in such a way that it may then become relevant, conspicuous and usable? Metaphoric expressions break from predetermined meanings in ways that invite interlocutors to participate in the creation of new forms of relation. One may wonder, for instance, what the infancy, parenting and ultimate senescence of humans would be like in the absence of just that non-literal, connective and initiatory language. Paradoxically, birth, reproduction and death in the human species would not be truly human with the sole aid of literal, conventional language; continually confronted with *that* sort of language, a human infant would hardly develop or else would 'evolve' into a sad imitation of a human being.

Of course, we can attempt to develop a synthesis by means of narratives, theories, new concepts, proverbs and metaphors, but we cannot be sure of its creative impact.[44] We could provisionally say that we have creativity when an individual or a group product generated within one disciplinary domain is regarded as innovative by its most credited representatives and sooner or later begins to influence subsequent achievements. But then, basically, one has to make connections that were not previously made. And, again, it takes a very special empathic force to make a connection that is creative, as contrasted with the sympathy that we naturally enact towards what is more familiar and easily coped with. The freedom to empathize with differing things and beings – as contrasted with our natural sympathy for whatever is sufficiently similar or familiar – could perhaps be illustrated by the creation of written language by the Sumerians. Even though pictograms existed at that time, the most these could do was to enumerate objects or depict situations; they could not be used to communicate abstract thoughts or complex objects – the visible and the invisible. The written tradition was initiated when we became capable of achieving an unprecedented connection between distinct signs and sounds, between two elements that do not resemble each other in the least. The gap that separates the use of pictograms and phonetic signs is, in fact, so great that we can regard the conjunction of graphic signs and sound vibrations as one of the major advances in the itinerary of hominization.

It is possible that the peaceful and agricultural Sumerians heeded the surrounding concert of nature and conversations so devotedly – in fact, empathically – as to recognize and appreciate the fascination of distinct, differing sounds. Perhaps the capacity to listen to a sound so accurately that it can become a specific vibration, an entity sufficiently differentiated from others, may have been the precondition for linking it to an identifying sign, thus inaugurating the immense perspective of our written tradition – from which we 'quickly' arrived at a telematic civilization.[45] What is essential is the connecting motion, our affective intention to link sounds and signs – our initiatory spontaneity in connecting them. From the present perspective of community making, we could perhaps remember that the admirable empathic capacity of the Sumerians seems to resonate through the centuries: in Galileo's *Dialogue on the Great World Systems*, the connectionist, empathic mentality is perhaps epitomized by Sagredus, who says: 'But above all other stupendous inventions, what sublimity of mind must have been his who conceived how to communicate his most secret thoughts to any other person, though very far distant either in time or place, speaking to those who are in the Indies, speaking to those who are not yet born, nor shall be this thousand, or ten thousand years? And with no greater difficulty than the various collocation of twenty-four little characters upon paper?'[46]

We are lately more inclined to speak about 'knowers' and 'scientists' than of 'the knower' and 'the scientist', even though the adoption of plural terms is not entirely deliberate and perhaps not clearly motivated. Indeed, the implausibility of 'epistemological individualism' is presented as a criticism of knowledge conceived as 'an individual affair . . . the mental activity of individual knowers grasping the one objective truth'.[47] A logic of epistemic communities gradually begins to prevail. In fact, Jaggar, Longino, Nelson and others have extensively argued that a solipsistic knower is implausible in light of human biology, and ethology, including neurobiology.[48] A further assumption underlying this outlook is that agents of knowledge are not isolated or isolable in the way of 'absolute' starting points, but they are deeply related and strongly connected agents. As Hankinson points out, even in the 'classicity' of mainstream philosophy there is some recognition that 'standards of evidence are historically relative and dynamic, emerging concomitantly with the processes through which knowledge is generated, rather than having been laid down prior to those processes'.[49]

The metaphoricity that is necessary for empathic connections is just not an automatic human phenomenon. Some individuals may have difficulties in the metaphoric transfer of significance or affects, and they may imitatively restrict themselves to the paths of whatever literal language is available in the micro- or macro-community; they seem unable to participate in the genius for the development of metaphoric links. We could think of human metaphoricity as the capacity to make connections and thus empathize with something that we previously regarded as alien or nonexistent. But then, the boundary between metaphor and nonsense frequently appears to be flexible; for indeed, if read literally, a metaphor would not make much sense, as its most salient characteristics are its semantic absurdity and its transgression of lexical rules. More precisely, metaphor violates the conditions governing normal applications of its terms by joining elements whose semantic markers are incompatible. In the celebrated Aristotelian definition, in fact, 'Metaphor consists in giving the thing a name that belongs to something else.'[50] And yet, however implausible this is, we could not properly function without metaphoric passages. Aristotle goes as far as 'proclaiming' that 'The greatest thing by far, is to be a master of metaphor. It is the one thing that cannot be learnt; and it is also a sign of genius.'[51] The relevance of the connective genius of human metaphoricity can be double-checked, perhaps, if we juxtapose the richness of metaphor to the plainness of conventional language. From the present perspective of community making, we could invoke the philosopher's reiterations that 'Slaves must speak *plainly* before their masters' and thus abstain from the genius of metaphor. He says: 'It is not quite appropriate that fine language should be used by a slave.'[52] But who is a 'slave'? If we regard the slave as an emblematic figure standing for whoever has insufficient contractual power in any given situation, standing for those excluded from any form of spontaneity, those whose psychic and rational existence is denied, then the injunction to avoid 'fine language' for making novel connections can be equated with the prohibition even to envisage changes in the dominant world view. And why should there be changes for 'slaves', once they are relegated into the domain of *natural* entities by only recognizing their physical and biological condition? The 'slave' is the emblematic figure about whom in olden times they could 'legitimately' say that 'He is' or 'He is not' such and such, without considering that he might be creatively evolving, indifferent to definition, *and* returning the epistemic gaze. Slaves being what 'they are', the 'citizens' could appropriately make use of their 'essential' being. Prohibiting them to use any 'fine' – metaphoric, paradoxical, analogic, poetic (poietic) – language is a way of ensuring that 'slaves' remain constrained in such a stable way that the burden of their submission does not weigh upon the masters but is conveniently placed upon the slaves themselves. It is thus a pre-emptive condition that they be persuaded to 'speak plainly', to avoid 'fine language' and keep their minds confined within one single vocabulary. Granting permission to address their 'superiors' through a 'fine language' would be comparable to recognizing the slaves' capacity to migrate from one epistemic context to another, where they could make new empathic contacts and new affectual investments; conversely, their 'own' (imposed) vocabulary should only be suited to producing self-fulfilling prophecies supporting the status quo from which they emanate.[53]

The best way to prevent the success of connective, empathic language is not to respond to any attempts in this direction; a stony silence would indicate that their 'fine language' is nonsense. In fact, exclusive reliance on the literalness of language conceals the danger of devaluing all those spontaneous attempts to expand contacts that can only be expressed metaphorically, and certainly not in terms of commensurable standards. Devaluation of these attempts seems an ordinary, invisible way of stifling empathy and inducing self-abjection. What we need instead is an outlook allowing for a transition from the cultural narcissism of isolated intra-commensurable phatic communities to a weaving of contacts connecting non-homogeneous domains. When there is talk of strangers with whom we cannot create bonds, authors tend to conjure up examples of absolute strangers such as extragalactics, 'savages', or 'slaves' in Aristotle's times. The hypothesis of such interlocutors is probably more comfortable than the idea of segregated parts of the mind, of our own mind. Ultimate strangers may be less disquieting than fellow speakers in our own phatic community, speaking from too-distant points in the life cycle, or from unacceptable pathologic styles.

The quality of the bonds within the community influences the sort of knowledge that is produced. Thus, the type of form of life that prevails ultimately influences our forms of knowledge. As human biology seems to indicate, an interdependency that undermines the self-sufficiency implicit in the modernist view of the 'self' has a bearing on what we know or could know. It is the growing recognition that it is micro- or macro-communities that develop and acquire knowledge, which counsels us to regard epistemic communities as the central agents of knowledge. But then, there are major difficulties in generating a communal life-enhancing synthesis. Even in our circumscribed disciplinary domains, it is difficult to try to think in a comprehensive way. It must therefore be even more arduous to reconnect a great variety of sources of information, perspectives and priorities in such a way that they may constitute a synthesis at the service of life.[54]

We tend to specialize, and become quite proficient in, one field of inter-active games, or of knowledge or of work. Thus, we become 'suspicious' of fields of expression that are incommensurable or sufficiently distant from our own. The question, of course, is which persons or institutions are competent enough to teach the art of making syntheses.[55] And also, even when the practice of synthesis is willed and cultivated, it is difficult to assess the fertility or productivity of a synthesis and to diagnose when it is premature or misleading – or unnecessary.

In Midgley's view, we should stop thinking of this entity called 'science' as an expanding empire, destined one day to take over the whole intellectual world.[56] Our current difficulties concerning the environment and inner well-being are problems that need cooperative work from the most disparate of disciplines. The intense academic specialization that prevails today makes this cooperation hard enough, without adding the extra obstacles imposed by an idealized notion of science. Especially in our times, an ability to weave together a coherent cluster of ever-increasing information deriving from the most disparate sources constitutes the critical factor for survival – psychic, individual and social. Sources of information are vast and incommensurable, while human beings relentlessly strive for integration and coherence. And so perhaps the most sought-after form of intelligence might be the capacity to attempt empathic, creative, syntheses.

Chapter 10

Self-formation and self-decreation

Why decreate our selves?

Just as we attach such tremendous importance to the innumerable ways towards self-formation, we should perhaps also appreciate the clinical relevance of self-decreation. This necessity of focusing on processes of deconstruction can only become evident, of course, if we can adopt a sufficiently perspectival outlook – that is, if we try to somehow bear in mind our entire life cycle. We could say that we are constantly intent on the tasks of self-formation and self-preservation, whereas the cultivation of spontaneity often seems to require self-decreation. Without this attitude of unconditional consent to otherness and time, all forms of 'heroism' or psychic marvels are still subject to the mechanisms of repetition and narcissistic falsification.

When considering our young ones, we all think that the sooner they engage in self-formation the better it is for their inner lives. The thesis here is a comparable one, in the sense that if we could think of some hypothetic point in time of accomplished self-formation, then the process of self-decreation should immediately be initiated, and not retarded; a delay in decreation would be as serious a problem as a delayed process of self-formation. Our well-formed selves may be regarded as the superb results of our struggles for psychic survival. And yet, once the masterwork has been accomplished it may go on 'functioning' indefinitely by means of the same relational policies, even to the point at which it can debilitate our personality. But then, the question is whether it would be possible to let go of it, or of parts of it. It is not a matter of giving up something 'false', however, but of giving up something that has been quite useful for psychic survival – and this is the distressing aspect of the process. The point is that to achieve a continuation of development in the course of life and to understand further what something really means for us, we have to sacrifice the way in which we have conceived of things up to now.[1] Our previous understanding does not obviously become 'false'; rather, it becomes insufficient for ulterior purposes. It is not disproved but must be renounced for the sake of further advances.

The need sometimes arises to step outside of a conventional scheme and risk a leap into the void, in order to escape the fixity of the inner structures that constrain us almost as strictly as do the signals of our instinctual nature. The hereditary load of programmes that in part determine our responses to otherness seems to assume a much lesser position in the face of an inner structure so 'well formed' and 'successful' that it finally tends to respond to nothing but itself. It is like an endless inner echo relayed from one part of the self to another, reverberating and rebounding through the same discourses. As we can readily observe, we sometimes appreciate that it is wonderful for somebody to develop into a successful person, but then we may secretly feel sorry for that person strenuously maintaining the contours of his psychic and social accomplishments. We could, for instance, think of some individuals who excel as clinicians, scholars and theorists and who reach a stellar position in a micro- or macro-community. It is possible that these subjects would greatly gain from a process of self-decreation as an alternative to becoming fixed or constrained in their interlocking personal and professional achievements. Such psycho-social conditions can ultimately be detrimental to spontaneity and transformation.

Our higher educational systems seem to be focused on the development of those skills associated with greater contractual value in a logocentric, logocratic society and are thus intent upon discrediting the values of inner spontaneity in the most drastic manner: by not even noticing its existence. The notions of power and strength are often used erroneously in our culture as though they were interchangeable terms.[2] But then, it is a lack of inner strength that in fact is trying to regain its balance through a search, as secret as it is unrestrainable, for power or for some link with power. The most archaic interactions seem to dominate in a culture as a result of the insufficient strength of our powerful egos, however admirable they may be in their expressive discourses. Our potential spontaneity may be suppressed by the despotic influence of success as well as by the self-imposed requirements established for the maintenance of success. One might even surmise that successful 'normality' is linked to a latent pathology involving as much falsification as consensus, and ultimately deafening the mind to those inner aspirations that run counter to the attained successful condition.

Once involved in a psychoanalytic process, patients do not always regard it as a precious opportunity to overcome character disabilities, but at times as though they were being encouraged to give something up or to part from something of which they do not want to be deprived. This attitude, of course, is due to the fact that over their long time adaptation this resistance made perfect sense, whereas from their current perspective it is not quite 'wrong' but perhaps simply uncertain: their pathology has in fact served them well, until the point when the life price became too high.[3] It is the very best that they could manage. The point is not, in Parsons' view, that this is how ill they are, but that this is how healthy they have managed to be.[4]

With this outlook, then, it makes good sense to try to hold on to our own masterwork of self-formation. Analysts believe that they are proposing a much better prospect, while analysands may have no good reason to believe in it. We could, for instance, invoke the case of a patient who lives in the conviction that he can only obtain the love of others by enchanting them with his brilliant argumentative skills; he knows of no other way of surviving psychically in spite of his difficulties in securing just the love he needs. Thus, he can only insist on enchanting the analyst and sees no reason to abandon this 'vital' part of the self. Yet while the analysand may gradually come to struggle to relinquish parts of his own self for the sake of a more rewarding adaptation, so must the analyst also strive to let go of his view of things for the sake of a new insight into the confrontation. In other words, the two of them – not just the patient – must be(come) capable of self-decreation.

Self-decreation is a subtractive process, one that is not enforced from the outside but is spontaneously generated for the sake of a more intense inner life, of a liberation from burdens hindering the continuing maturation of the self. To word it in an extreme way: we may regret the afflictions that demolish obsolete parts of the self from the outside because, after that, we can no longer let go of them ourselves – spontaneously.

Even though influenced by external conditions and biological inheritance, self-formation is also influenced by the heavy demands of the story that the individual has created for himself and is constantly trying to revise. The story itself relies on assumptions, or psychic stipulations, that function almost like a genetic grammar in the process of self-development. Defensive assumptions can often be identified that guide one's journey by shaping a diachronic, enduring structure. Repeated attempts to tell one's life story not only constitute accounts, given in the here and now, of events that took place in the there and then; in the endeavour of recounting one's story, the narrator and the protagonist tend to actually coincide in the 'end', an end that functions as an inaugural opportunity for re-examining the underlying assumptions sustaining the self.[5] At the 'end' of the story, connective links can perhaps be identified that dictate for us what our basic attitudes to otherness should be. As such connecting structures become less obscure, the subject may also uncover the guidelines of his itinerary that have been hidden so far. At this point, these may even come to appear as devoided of their promises, or false, banal and disposable – ready to be given up. One should, of course, be sufficiently attracted to giving up certain established modes of seeking sense and satisfaction for the purpose of making innovative investments that run contrary to acquired habits; this attraction should be strong enough for us to open inner routes for both self-renovation and decreation.

Klein, at her most pessimistic, viewed pathological greed as an irremovable constitutive trait that is not responsive to maturational processing.

And yet, it could be illuminating to address the problem[6] of oral greed by regarding it as an expression of resistance to processes of separation, loss and differentiation. We could think that the developing person's physiological life provides opportunities to live through experiences of separation and change: the inexorable return of the state of hunger tells the infant that what is eaten will not become his forever. Similarly, the affectual voracity of certain subjects might be interpreted as a desperate attempt to suppress the whole experience of need, with a view to escaping the fearsome awareness of temporariness, separation and loss.[7] It seems almost as if certain creatures are entertaining the hope that if only their efforts for oral satisfaction were to succeed, they would remain forever satiated, in a comfortable state of union with some re-edition of primal holding.

The main impediment to making use of new levels of consciousness is the attachment to what is 'old', to a long-standing relational attitude; by attitude, or position, we could mean an affective propensity to act or to react selectively in response to certain aspects of another person. Just as symbolic thought may be developed solely through a process of mourning – or working through of loss – so also the changes necessitated by creative life and spontaneity may be implemented primarily when one achieves the ability to discard something, almost a part of one's own self, or a basic affectual assumption for which the individual may have developed a sort of addiction. In fact, what we should often do is to give up an explicative hypothesis that is constantly and unwittingly introduced whenever we address a problem we have with others, and which makes it impossible to solve the problem. Paradoxically, there seems to be an increasing number of confrontations in life when a propensity for self-decreation is more life-enhancing than our capacity for safeguarding whatever form of self we have developed. As is known, a passively introjected, imploded view of one's own self may tend to function as a self-fulfilling prophecy. Through a more spontaneous attitude of monitoring the inner prophecies that fulfil themselves, our capacity for eschewing them might be optimized. In fact, a metaphoric prophecy that we can diagnose as just an imploded metaphor – such as 'I am a ____', or 'I am just a ____' – could not properly fulfil itself: it would feel too obsolete to be kept alive. As soon as a 'trick' becomes clear, we are no longer bound to a naïve way of playing the game, and no longer constrained by it.[8] We can let go of it. The richness of life and interactions may constantly be defying our previous defensive (or not so defensive) constructions. Should such richness be tacitly denied by constantly endorsing the ultimate value of our constitutive 'convictions', the individual constrained by it would tend to be excluded from life itself, inasmuch as a caricature of reality would come to be enforced.

In our early experiences, the resources and potential for psychic life somehow tend to become ciphered, identified, in their ways of guiding behaviour. They may become the 'metaphors we live by'.[9] By silently accepting a metaphor more in the way of a passive implosion than in the way of internalization, one may absorb a particular way of seeing the world, a way of focusing on something that 'really' matters; alternatively one may establish a pre-emptive closure for the potential existence of consequential psychic functions. Deriving from a joint process of construction and construals, our metaphors establish – or annul – prospects for further dimensions of our psychic life. In fact, we actually understand some metaphoric 'principle' by participating in its vision. And even when the vision is actually a damaging cause of blindness, we may accept the damage for the sake of preserving our sense of belonging in some particular community (our participation in construals). But then, as we gradually relinquish this burning desire to belong, when we are ready to partially die socially, we may concurrently break free from our blinding factors. In this sense, the process of self-decreation becomes essential for our growth in spontaneity. We could think of the attempts at decreation as healthy ways of decolonizing our own self and of abandoning attitudes that we can let go of.

With candour and clarity the philosopher Bacon points out that 'The human understanding when it has once adopted an opinion . . . draws all things else to support and agree with it. And though there be a greater number and weight of instances to be found on the other side, yet these it either neglects and despises, or else by some distinction sets aside and rejects, in order that by this great and pernicious predetermination the authority of the former conclusions may remain inviolate.'[10] In the life-enhancing deconstruction of our selves, we learn to gladly accept these violations.

Letting go of the self

As the passage of time or the closing of a life cycle are topics that are usually too difficult to think about, the ultimate result is not only a delusion of eternity but also a withdrawal from the full use of life. Conversely, to the extent that we can think of our finitude and of giving up features of our own self, we may gain the ability to make use of that part of our human condition that would otherwise disappear into a current of unfathomable fearfulness. Jung's synthetic acumen would seem to provide support for this approach: 'The negation of life's fulfilment is synonymous with the refusal to accept its ending. Both mean not wanting to live, and not wanting to live is identical with not wanting to die. . . . Whenever possible our consciousness refuses to accommodate itself to this undeniable truth.'[11]

There is an intellectual need to keep all relational forms locked within the grid of the better-known and easily accessible epistemologies – that is, there is a desire to always know and so control what is going on, even at the risk of impeding knowledge. These attitudes stand in the way not only of any labour of loss (or death, at the extreme) but also of the travail of our human genius, of our ordinary, daily genius.[12] Should a climate of cognitive constriction prevail, it may induce a sense of paralysis that hinders the life of thought and even prevents us from living the often extremely lengthy ending of our lives. In this unspontaneous way, the experience of death may take on the conventional appearance of an absurd future mishap, never to be mentioned for any reason – or only by necessity. The mental muteness that enforces a stereotyped set of blind spots not only obscures the awareness of death, but also impedes the development of our spontaneity. Whereas the knowing subject will always balk at letting himself die, dying cognitively amounts to giving up the more powerful vocabulary in order to tap into inner sources, and thus no longer relying on existing routes or mechanisms. It is not possible, in fact, to have or to acquire a propensity for self-renovation, or to seek it imitatively. An insane inner logic might otherwise prevail in which 'having' can be passed off as 'being'. And the labour of spontaneity does not tread well-worn psychic paths; it develops, instead, through an inner attitude springing from the knowing acceptance of our interlocking experiences of death and birth. As the only form of life capable of living in the awareness of time, and of somehow knowing about death, those who do not attain a sufficient spontaneity have to pretend not to know, and then pretend that they are not pretending, and so forth – in a damaging spiral.

Possibly one way of defending oneself against the ubiquitous obscuration of death may be found in the demystifying efforts whereby we create psychic spaces in which we attempt pursuits such as 'the work of mourning' and the experience of loss – not only for the loss of our famous objects but also, ultimately, for the loss of parts of our own self. An awareness of our inevitable ending is, in fact, a remarkable step forward, however difficult to entertain as a thought. One may even wonder if so 'evanescent' an idea of our finite condition is worth keeping, and thus we are tempted to cast it into oblivion by avoiding the effort to symbolize it in any way. Our human condition is, in fact, that of mortal beings who are not quite able to say how they fit within a finite temporal frame and who become forced all the more to deny, ignore and disclaim. But then, if we view death as an essential aspect of life, it follows that any attitude that colludes with the multifarious ways in which it is denied will even hinder and falsify the *essential* quality of our psychic experiences. The ability to relinquish certain intellectual functions – virtually a capacity to let oneself die mentally, to plummet out of a grid of intelligibility – is a capacity that in some way is provided by one's sufficiently developed sense of subjective agency. For it would not be easy for an individual to silence standard logic if this meant running the risk of disintegrating inwardly; it would not be possible to let go and come out of the constricted spaces of what is consensually knowable if this ultimately did not enhance the birth of new, enlivening thoughts.

As is known, one of the 'psychoanalytic' perversions could reside in the temptation of omniscience. This may at times even masquerade as an inquisitive, perspicacious mind. As we know, people may behave oddly and we will not understand why; things may go unexpectedly wrong – or right – and it will not make sense to us. There will always be predicaments that we cannot understand, and our incapacity to just accept this might even debilitate our subjective agency. People do not always make sense, just as life does not always make sense. We will never understand everything, and the propensity to illusorily believe that we can is the asphyxiating product of our self-perpetuating selves. If we cannot understand, we can psychically give up; we could make a choice of renunciation rather than letting the incomprehensible situation parasite us through the illusion of our cognitive control over it.

There is, of course, literature on our tenacious inclination to use denial as a defensive measure. Still, if we assume that anything that is denied, or glossed over, will re-emerge in distorted form, we shall be motivated to explore our reluctance to cope with our finitude, a reluctance that possibly reinforces the falsifying currents threatening our inner life. We cannot ignore that, whatever our socio-biological well-being, there are inclinations to destructiveness that are expressed through disparate, more or less conspicuous styles of violence directed both at others and at ourselves. Just as in years past selective blindness and denial produced the taboos surrounding our human Eros, in the same way we are now witnessing a pervasive tendency to make a taboo of both destructiveness and death itself. And while death is not acceptable or thinkable, it still gains our 'cultural' stage in its distorted, commercial, exciting pornography. Our culture denies death while going on feeding insatiably on a motley assortment of entertainments based on misrepresentations of our human finitude. Even 'horror', for instance, sells quite profitably. There are not enough logical spaces in our culture and minds suitable for containing and rendering thinkable what is generally regarded as unthinkable, and it is thus represented in caricatures or distortions.

Any creative process appears to be the result of the ability to set vicissitudes in motion that are at the same time contrasting and complementary: activeness and passivity, orientation and bewilderment. And, of course, the genius of our human creativity does not refer here to the artistic or scientific achievements documented in our cultural heritage. The creativity that concerns us here is our capacity for psychic survival, coexistence and responsibility. A glance at the phases of human creative ventures seems to confirm the interactive, interdependent nature of antithetic human propensities. We might envisage a necessary connection between our ordinary genius and a paradoxical human capacity to both use and relinquish our cognitive power. At some point in the maturational process, the ability to set aside the use of our intellectual functions appears to become downright indispensable, almost as if facing the risk of not knowing, or of losing control, were a necessary step in pursuing spontaneity. In other words, reflexive breakdown is important because it is a disruption of our capacity to be self-interpreting creatures. It also represents a peculiar kind of irrationality, because what we are able to say or think about ourselves seems to be contradicted by what we strive to do;[13] perhaps we cannot bear to let crises affect our 'wonderful' established selves.

Whenever one is anxious, one becomes even more anxious about precipitating further in this condition, and whenever depressed, more depressed over being so afflicted. And yet we may gradually 'learn' how not to be afraid of being helpless when we are most fragile, how to allow ourselves to be dependent and not self-reliant when we can no longer cope. The problem is that we cannot easily abandon parts of our selves, constitutive aspects and basic assumptions: 'Big boys don't cry.' It may look like an unbearable loss of power. It is ironic that we should abhor what may also function as a vital passage. Spontaneity is not linked to power and does not protect the psyche against the coldness of blows. Only an imaginary and idolized attachment, if it carries enough power, can afford protection against crisis. If we want a 'love' that will protect the soul from wounds, we must avoid openness and instead find cultural conglomerations that more closely match with the inner idols presiding over our changelessness. According to Eigen, being helpless is more scandalous than being promiscuous. With all the acknowledgement that we are simply human, there is still the ominous dictate that we must have power and that there must be nothing wrong.[14] Which decent self could be 'wrong'? The sense that something may be dying inside us has, of course, been voiced in major literature through the ages. Oedipus' acknowledgement that there is an epidemic in the town, or Hamlet's talk about something rotten in the state, could be transferred from the social context to the individual condition.

Even our psychoanalytic culture is not entirely free from incitements to lasting power. The language of our founding fathers resonates with allusions to colonization and expansion, such as rendering fit for cultivation those territories in which previously nothing but madness had grown, penetrating with the sharpened axe of reason in order to fortify the Ego and perfect its organization so that it can annex new areas of the Id. But then, the thesis that runs through the present work is, of course, that both as individuals and as a species we have more to gain from accepted vulnerability than from illusory power.

Notes

1 Introductory remarks

1 A comparable suggestion is discussed in Kelly Oliver, *The Colonization of Psychic Space: A Psychoanalytic Social Theory of Oppression*, Minneapolis, MN/ London: University of Minnesota Press, 2004, p. 199.
2 This thesis is elaborated in Gemma Corradi Fiumara, 'The fragility of "pure reason"', in *The Mind's Affective Life: A Psychoanalytic and Philosophical Inquiry*, London/New York: Brunner-Routledge, 2001, chapter 1, pp. 4–19.
3 This point is also addressed by Julia Kristeva, *New Maladies of the Soul*, trans. Ross Guberman, New York: Columbia University Press, 1995, p. 90.
4 Stephen Mitchell says: 'Some believe that "primitive" instinctual sexuality or destructiveness is at the core of primordial human experience, others also assume a delicate, easily bruised creativity.' *Hope and Dread in Psychoanalysis*, New York: Basic Books, 1993, p. 42.
5 See Neville Symington, *Narcissism: A New Theory*, London, Karnac, 1993, p. 8.
6 See Christopher Bollas, *The Forces of Destiny: Psychoanalysis and Human Idiom*, London: Free Association Books, 1991.
7 Neville Symington, *A Pattern of Madness*, London: Karnac, 2002, p. 33.
8 Erich Fromm, *The Fear of Freedom* (1942), London/New York: Routledge, 2005, p. 222.
9 Symington, *Narcissism*, p. 93, emphasis added.
10 Ricardo Bernardi, 'The role of paradigmatic determinants in psychoanalytic understanding', *International Journal of Psychoanalysis*, 1995, vol. 70, pp. 341–57.
11 P. A. Schilpp and L. E. Hahn (eds.), *The Philosophy of Georg Henrik von Wright*, La Salle, IL: Open Court Press, 1989, p. 843.
12 This topic is developed in section 3, 'Mind-like idols', of Chapter 2, 'Rethinking internalization'.
13 Sigmund Freud, 'On narcissism', *Standard Edition*, 1914, vol. 14, p. 91.
14 Roy Schaefer, *A New Language for Psychoanalysis*, New Haven, CT: Yale University Press, 1978.
15 Jonathan Lear, *Open Minded: Working Out the Logic of the Soul*, Cambridge, MA: Harvard University Press, 1998.
16 Symington, *Narcissism*, p. 4.
17 This issue is discussed in section 1, 'From the mechanics of reaction to the spontaneity of action', of Chapter 6, 'Actions and reactions'.
18 Sigmund Freud, 'Review of August Forel's *Hypnotism*', *Standard Edition*, 1889, vol. 1, p. 94.

19 Sigmund Freud, *Psychopathology of Everyday Life*, chapter 12, 'Determinism, belief in chance and superstition – [on] some points of view', *Standard Edition*, 1901, vol. 6, p. 253.
20 John McDowell, *Mind and World*, Cambridge, MA: Harvard University Press, 1994 [*Mente e mondo*, Turin: Einaudi, 1994, Lecture 4, p. 81].
21 See Georg Henrik von Wright, *Of Human Freedom in the Shadow of Descartes*, Dordrecht: Kluwer, 1998, pp. 30–32. See also Rosaria Egidi, 'G.H. von Wright on self determination and free agency', in E. Niiniluoto and R. Vilkko (eds.), *Philosophical Essays in Memoriam George Henrik von Wright*, Acta Philosophica Phennica [Helsinki], 2005, vol. 77, pp. 105–14.
22 Ana-Maria Rizzuto, W. W. Meissner and Dan H. Buie, *The Dynamics of Human Aggression: Theoretical Foundations, Clinical Implications*, New York/Hove: Brunner-Routledge, 2004, p. 82.
23 Symington, *Narcissism*, p. 108.
24 Oliver, *Colonization of Psychic Space*, p. 8.

2 Rethinking internalization

1 In this connection see, for instance, 'The Oedipus Complex in the light of early anxieties', in Melanie Klein, *Contributions to Psycho-Analysis 1921–1945*, ed. Ernest Jones, London: Hogarth Press and the Institute of Psycho-Analysis, 1973, pp. 339–90.
2 Sigmund Freud, *The Origins of Psycho-Analysis: Letters to Wilhelm Fliess, Drafts and Notes, 1887–1902*, eds. M. Bonaparte, A. Freud and E. Kriss, London, Imago: 1954; Letter 69, pp. 215 ff.
3 Michael Parsons, *The Dove that Returns, The Dove that Vanishes: Paradox and Creativity in Psychoanalysis*, The New Library of Psychoanalysis, London: Routledge, 2000, p. 37.
4 Haidée Faimberg, *Ascoltando tre generazioni. Legami narcisistici e identificazioni alienanti*, Milan: Franco Angeli, 2000, pp. 134–5.
5 Eugenio Gaddini, 'On imitation', *International Journal of Psychoanalysis*, 1969, vol. 50, pp. 475–84 [Summary].
6 Neville Symington, *Narcissism: A New Theory*, London: Karnac, 1993, p. 4.
7 Ibid.
8 Charles Altieri, *Subjective Agency: A Theory of First-Person Expressivity and Its Social Implications*, Oxford, UK/Cambridge, MA: Blackwell Publishers, 1994, p. 4.
9 James Strachey, 'The nature of the therapeutic action of psycho-analysis', *International Journal of Psycho-Analysis*, 1934, vol. 15, pp. 127–59.
10 Neville Symington, *A Pattern of Madness*, London: Karnac, 2002, p. 67.
11 There is an expanding literature on the topic of *Nachträglichkeit*, variously referred to as 'deferred effect', 'retranscription of memory', 're-categorization of experience', and 'retrospective attribution'. Freud perhaps was not prepared to fully develop this seminal line of inquiry; indeed, his presentation of *Nachträglichkeit* is hinted at in different parts of his numerous works; as early as 1896 the idea was expressed in a letter to Fliess. 'I should like to emphasize the fact that the successive registrations represent the psychic achievement of successive epochs of life. At the boundary between two such epochs a translation of the psychic material must take place.' Letter dated 6 December 1896, J. Masson (ed.), *The Complete Letters of Sigmund Freud to Wilhelm Fliess*, Cambridge, MA: Harvard University Press, 1985, p. 207.
12 See Neville Symington, *The Spirit of Sanity*, London: Karnac, 2001, p. 162.

13 Ibid., p. 161.
14 See Joyce McDougall, *The Many Faces of Eros: A Psychoanalytic Exploration of Human Sexuality*, London: Free Association Books, 1995, p. 233.
15 Gaddini, 'On imitation', pp. 475–84.
16 Hermann Hesse, *La nevrosi si può vincere*, Italian trans. by Oreste Bernardi, Milan: Mondatori, 1997, p. 45.
17 Roberta De Monticelli, *L'ordine del cuore: Etica e teoria del sentire*, Milan: Garzanti, 2003, p. 278.
18 Symington, *Spirit of Sanity*, p. 115.
19 Wilfred R. Bion, 'A theory of thinking', *International Journal of Psychoanalysis*, 1962, vol. 43, pp. 306–10.
20 Gaddini, 'On imitation', pp. 475–84.
21 Symington, *Narcissism*, p. 20.
22 Carl Gustav Jung, 'The Tavistock Lectures – Lecture III', in *The Collected Works of C. G. Jung*, vol. 18, *The Symbolic Life*, London: Routledge & Kegan Paul, 1977, pp. 72–3.
23 Joyce McDougall, *Theatres of the Mind: Illusion and Truth on the Psychoanalytic Stage*, London: Free Association Books, 1986, p. 4.
24 Ibid., p. 7.
25 Otto Kernberg, 'Foreword', in McDougall, *Theatres of the Mind*, p. x.
26 Jonathan Lear, *Open Minded: Working out the Logic of the Soul*, Cambridge, MA: Harvard University Press, 1998, p. 82.
27 See Gemma Corradi Fiumara, 'From philosophy to epistemophily', in *The Mind's Affective Life: A Psychoanalytic and Philosophical Inquiry*, London/New York: Brunner-Routledge, chapter 2, pp. 20–32.
28 Patrick Casement, *Learning from Our Mistakes: Beyond Dogma in Psychoanalysis and Psychotherapy*, London/New York: Brunner-Routledge, 2004, p. 12.
29 Søren Kierkegaard, *The Sickness unto Death: A Christian Psychological Exposition for Upbuilding and Awakening* (1849), ed. Howard V. Hong and Edna H. Hong, Princeton, NJ: Princeton University Press, 1983, p. 13.
30 Francis Bacon, *The Advancement of Learning and New Atlantis*, ed. Arthur Johnson, Oxford: Clarendon Press, 1974, p. 127.
31 Gaddini, 'On Imitation', p. 475.
32 This topic is extensively explored in Gemma Corradi Fiumara, *The Symbolic Function: Psychoanalysis and the Philosophy of Language*, especially chapter 7, 'Pseudosymbolic Language', Oxford, UK/Cambridge, MA: Blackwell Publishers, 1992, pp. 80–108.
33 Bacon, *Advancement of Learning*, p. 127.
34 Piera Aulagnier, *The Violence of Interpretation: From Pictogram to Statement*, trans. Alan Sheridan, The New Library of Psychoanalysis, London/New York: Brunner-Routledge, 2001.
35 Jung, 'Tavistock Lectures', pp. 72–3 (emphasis added).
36 Symington, *Pattern of Madness*, p. 123.
37 Ibid., p. 38.
38 Casement, *Learning from Our Mistakes*, p. xv.
39 Kaja Silverman, *The Threshold of the Visible World*, London/New York: Routledge, 1996, p. 40.
40 McDougall, *Theatres of the Mind*, p. 10.

3 The function of paradox

1 Nicholas Rescher, *Paradoxes: Their Roots, Range and Resolution*, Chicago/La Salle, IL: Open Court Publishing Company, 2001, p. 3

2 Sigmund Freud, 'Observations on transference-love', *Standard Edition*, 1915, vol. 12, pp. 157–71.

3 Arnold Modell, 'The therapeutic relationship as a paradoxical experience', *Psychoanalytic Dialogue*, 1991, vol. 1, pp. 13–28. Quoted in Stuart Pizer, *Building Bridges: The Negotiation of Paradox in Psychoanalysis*, Hillsdale, NJ/London: Analytic Press, p. xi.

4 The probable neologism 'psychopoietic' is used to indicate vicissitudes (comparable to inner metabolic processes) that essentially sustain and contribute to the formation of our psyche.

5 Pizer, *Building Bridges*, p. 140.

6 Michael Eigen, *Toxic Nourishment*, London: Karnac, 1999, p. 79.

7 Pizer, *Building Bridges*, p. 52.

8 It seems indeed the achievement of 'a proud man, most ignorant of what he is most assured, his glassy essence', William Shakespeare, *Measure for Measure*.

9 Pizer, *Building Bridges*, p. 140.

10 Donald Winnicott, *Playing and Reality*, London: Tavistock Publications, 1971. The concept is reiterated throughout the book.

11 J. M. Kumin, 'Developmental aspects of opposites and paradox', *International Review of Psychoanalysis*, 1978, vol. 5, pp. 477–84.

12 Herbert Rosenfeld frequently elaborated on this clinical assumption in the course of the regular seminars he conducted at the Rome Institute of Psychoanalysis (Centro Psicoanalitico di Roma) between 1975 and 1985.

13 Stephen Mitchell, *Hope and Dread in Psychoanalysis*, New York: Basic Books, 1993, p. 96.

14 Pizer, *Building Bridges*, p. 141.

15 Winnicott, *Playing and Reality*, p. xii.

16 Michael Eigen, 'The area of faith in Winnicott, Lacan and Bion', *International Journal of Psychoanalysis*, 1981, vol. 62, pp. 413–33.

17 Simone Weil, *Gravity and Grace* (1947), trans. Emma Crawford and Mario von der Ruhr, London/New York: Routledge Classics, 2007, p. 31.

18 Winnicott, *Playing and Reality*, p. 2.

19 Michael Parsons, 'The logic of play in psychoanalysis', *International Journal of Psychoanalysis*, 1999, vol. 80, pp. 871–84.

20 Winnicott, *Playing and Reality*, p. 38.

21 Eric Rayner, 'Infinite experiences, affects and the characteristics of the unconscious', *International Journal of Psychoanalysis*, 1981, vol. 65, pp. 403–12.

22 Neville Symington, *Narcissism: A New Theory*, London, Karnac, 1993, p. 40.

23 Michael Parsons, *The Dove that Returns, the Dove that Vanishes: Paradox and Creativity in Psychoanalysis*, The New Library of Psychoanalysis, London: Routledge, 2000, p. 131.

24 Eigen, *Toxic Nourishment*, p. 50.

25 Pizer, *Building Bridges*, p. 2.

26 Symington, *Narcissism*, p. 101.

27 Rescher, *Paradoxes*, p. 9.

28 Pizer, *Building Bridges*, p. 66.

29 Ludwig Wittgenstein, *Last Writings on the Philosophy of Psychology*, vol. II, *The Inner and the Outer, 1949–1951*, ed. G. H. von Wright and H. Nyman, trans. C. G. Luckhardt and M. A. E. Ane, Oxford: Basil Blackwell, 1992, paragraph 22e.

30 Pizer, *Building Bridges*, p. 65.

31 See Rescher, *Paradoxes*, p. 20.
32 On this point, see Pizer, *Building Bridges*, p. 178.
33 This concept was reiterated by Herbert Rosenfeld in the course of his regular Rome seminars from 1975 to 1985.
34 Pizer, *Building Bridges*, p. 159.
35 Ibid., p. 52.
36 Jessica Benjamin, *Shadow of the Other: Intersubjectivity and Gender in Psychoanalysis*, London: Routledge, 1998, p. 105.
37 Pizer, *Building Bridges*, p. xii.
38 Symington, *Narcissism*, p. 20.
39 Wittgenstein, *Last Writings*, paragraph 22e.
40 Pizer, *Building Bridges*, p. 71.
41 Donald Winnicott, *The Maturational Processes and the Facilitating Environment*, New York: International Universities Press, 1965, p. 61.
42 Eigen, *Toxic Nourishment*, p. 225.
43 Gustave Thibon, 'Introduction', in Simone Weil, *Gravity and Grace*, p. xxix.
44 Richard Feinman, *The Pleasure of Finding Things Out*, New York: Penguin Books, 2001, p. 248.

4 Subjective agency – *and* passivity

1 See, for instance, Wilfred R. Bion, *Transformations: Change from Learning to Growth*, London: Heinemann, 1965; *Attention and Interpretation: A Scientific Approach to Insight in Psycho-Analysis and Groups*, London: Tavistock, 1970.
2 Sigmund Freud, 'Lines of advance in psycho-analytic therapy', *Standard Edition*, 1919 [1918], vol. 17, p. 161.
3 Jessica Benjamin, *Shadow of the Other: Intersubjectivity and Gender in Psychoanalysis*, London: Routledge, 1998, p. 75.
4 Neville Symington, *Narcissism: A New Theory*, London: Karnac, 1993, p. 92.
5 Frances Tustin, *Autism and Childhood Psychosis*, London: Hogarth Press, 1972, p. 10.
6 Julia Kristeva, *New Maladies of the Soul*, trans. Ross Guberman, New York: Columbia University Press, 1995, pp. 5–6.
7 Donald Winnicott, *Playing and Reality*, London: Tavistock Publications, 1971, p. 53.
8 This suggestion is reiterated in several of his books.
9 Simone Weil, *Gravity and Grace* (1947), trans. Emma Crawford and Mario von der Ruhr, London/New York: Routledge Classics, 2007, p. 10.
10 Symington, *Narcissism*, pp. 92–3.
11 See Gemma Corradi Fiumara, *The Mind's Affective Life: A Psychoanalytic and Philosophical Inquiry*, London/New York: Brunner-Routledge, 2002.
12 Jessica Benjamin, *Shadow of the Other: Intersubjectivity and Gender in Psychoanalysis*, London: Routledge, 1998, p 87.
13 Neville Symington, *A Pattern of Madness*, London, Karnac, 2002, p. 26.
14 See Gemma Corradi Fiumara, *The Symbolic Function: Psychoanalysis and the Philosophy of Language*, Oxford, UK/Cambridge, MA: Blackwell Publishers, 1992. See especially chapter 10, 'Genesis of the symbolic function', pp. 135–53, and chapter 11, 'From Biological Life to Dialogic Relations', pp. 154–78.
15 Symington, *Pattern of Madness*, p. 185.
16 Symington, *Narcissism*, p. 120.

17 Salimbene de Adam of Parma, 'Chronicon Parmense. Avvenimenti tra il il 1167 e il 1287', in Antonio Viscardi *et al.* (eds.), *La letteratura italiana: Storia e testi: Le origini*, Milan/Naples: Ricciardi Editore, 1946, p. 979.
18 Roberta De Monticelli, *L'ordine del cuore: Etica e teoria del sentire*, Milan: Garzanti, 2003, p. 260.
19 Dante Alighieri, *The Inferno of Dante Alighieri. Inferno, Canto IX*, verses 55–60, London/New York: J.M. Dent & Sons, and Aldine House, 1958, p. 95.
20 See Gemma Corradi Fiumara, *The Other Side of Language: A Philosophy of Listening*, London/New York: Routledge, 1990, especially chapter 6, 'The philosophical problem of benumbment', pp. 72–81.
21 Corradi Fiumara, *Mind's Affective Life*, especially chapter 12, 'Affects and indifference', pp. 138–48.
22 De Monticelli, *L'ordine del cuore*, p. 267.
23 Jessica Benjamin, *Shadow of the Other: Intersubjectivity and Gender in Psychoanalysis*, London: Routledge, 1998, p. 75.
24 De Monticelli, *L'ordine del cuore*, p. 268.
25 Søren Kierkegaard, *The Sickness unto Death: A Christian Psychological Exposition for Upbuilding and Awakening* (1849), ed. and trans. Howard V. Hong and Edna H. Hong, Princeton, NJ: Princeton University Press, 1983, p. 18.
26 Symington, *Pattern of Madness*, p. 63.
27 Symington, *Narcissism*, p. 116.
28 Roy Schaefer, *A New Language for Psychoanalysis*, New Haven, CT/London: Yale University Press, 1976, p. 8.
29 Kristeva, *New Maladies of the Soul*, p. 9.
30 Jonathan Lear, *Open Minded: Working Out the Logic of the Soul*, Cambridge, MA: Harvard University Press, 1998, p. 3.
31 Ibid.
32 Ibid.
33 Ibid., p. 4.
34 Ibid.
35 Michael Eigen, *Toxic Nourishment*, London, Karnac, 1999, p. xiii.
36 Ibid.
37 Christopher Bollas, *Cracking Up: The Work of Unconscious Experience*, London: Routledge, 1997, pp. 97–8.
38 Ibid., p. 98.
39 See Corradi Fiumara, *Other Side of Language*, chapter 10, 'Midwifery and Philosophy', pp. 143–68.
40 Michael Eigen, 'The area of faith in Winnicott, Lacan and Bion', *International Journal of Psychoanalysis*, 1981, vol. 62, pp. 413–33.
41 Ibid., p. 430.
42 See Corradi Fiumara, *Symbolic Function*, chapter 10, 'From Biological Life to Dialogic Relations', pp. 154–78.
43 Donald Winnicott, *Playing and Reality*, New York: Basic Books, 1971, p. 70, emphasis added.
44 Marion Milner (as Joanna Field), *A Life of One's Own* (1934), London: Virago, 1986, p. 186.
45 Eigen, *Toxic Nourishment*, p. 172.
46 Ibid. Here Eigen is referring to one of Winnicott's hypotheses contained in *Psychoanalytic Explorations*, ed. C. Winnicott, R. Shepherd, and M. Davis, Cambridge, MA: Harvard University Press, 1989, p. 128.

47 See Corradi Fiumara, *Symbolic Function*; this issue is elaborated throughout the book.
48 Arnold Modell, *The Private Self*, Cambridge, MA/London: Harvard University Press, 1996, p. 71.
49 Ibid.
50 See Corradi Fiumara, *Mind's Affective Life*, pp. 20–32, for a discussion of the distinction between epistemology and epistemophily.
51 Modell, *Private Self*, p. 75.
52 James Strachey, 'The nature of the therapeutic action of psycho-analysis', *International Journal of Psycho-Analysis*, 1934, vol. 15, pp. 127–59.
53 See Francis Bacon, *The Advancement of Learning and the New Atlantis*, ed. Arthur Johnston, Oxford: Clarendon Press, 1974.
54 Friedrich Nietzsche, *Genealogia della Morale*, 'Seconda dissertazione', trans. and ed. F. Masini, G. Colli and M. Montanari, in *Opere di Friedrich Nietzsche*, vol. VI, book II, Milan: Adelphi, 1976, p. 255.
55 Paul Ricoeur, *Sé come un altro*, trans. Daniella Jannotta, Milan: Jaca Book, 1993, pp. 79–102.
56 Herbert Rosenfeld reiteratively elaborated on this issue in the course of his regular seminars given at the Rome Institute of Psychoanalysis (Centro Psicoanalitico di Roma) between 1975 and 1985.
57 These neologisms have already been used in Corradi Fiumara, *Mind's Affective Life*, p. 141.
58 See Naomi Scheman, *Engenderings: Constructions of Knowledge, Authority and Privilege*, London/New York: Routledge, 1993, p. 69.
59 Kaja Silverman, *The Threshold of the Visible World*, London/New York: Routledge, 1996, p. 40.
60 Robert Caper, 'A mind of one's own', *International Journal of Psychoanalysis*, vol. 78(2), 1997, pp. 265–78.
61 See Corradi Fiumara, *Mind's Affective Life*, pp. 4–16.
62 Caper, 'A Mind of One's Own'.
63 Scheman, *Engenderings*, p. 86.
64 Corradi Fiumara, *Mind's Affective Life*, p. 141.
65 Michael Parsons, *The Dove that Returns, the Dove that Vanishes: Paradox and Creativity in Psychoanalysis*, The New Library of Psychoanalysis, London: Routledge, 2000, p. 1.
66 Christopher Bollas, *The Forces of Destiny: Psychoanalysis and Human Idiom*, London: Free Association Books, 1991; see chapters 1 and 2.
67 Parsons, *The Dove that Returns*, pp. 33–4.
68 Eigen, *Toxic Nourishment*, p. 216.
69 Kierkegaard, *Sickness unto Death*, p. 86.
70 Joseph Epstein, *Envy: The Seven Deadly Sins*, Oxford: Oxford University Press, 2003, p. 21.
71 Ibid., p. 11.
72 Symington, *Narcissism*, p. 48.
73 *Genesis*, 11: 1 9.
74 Epstein, *Envy*, p. xxiv.
75 Jacqueline Rose, *On Not Being Able to Sleep: Psychoanalysis and the Modern World*, London: Vintage, 2004, p. 4.
76 Melanie Klein, *Envy and Gratitude*, London: Tavistock Publications, 1957. See also *Contributions to Psycho-Analysis 1921–1945*, ed. Ernest Jones, London: Hogarth Press and The Institute of Psycho-Analysis, 1973, especially pp. 209–11, 271–2, 384–5.

77 Epstein, *Envy*, p. 15.
78 Neville Symington, *Spirit of Sanity*, London: Karnac, 2001, p. 185.
79 Epstein, *Envy*, p. 79.
80 Ibid., p. 78.
81 Ibid.
82 Rose, *On Not Being Able to Sleep*, p. 12.
83 Ibid., p. 13.
84 Ibid.
85 Ibid.
86 Ibid.
87 Kelly Oliver, *The Colonization of Psychic Space: A Psychoanalytic Social Theory of Oppression*, Minneapolis, MN/London: University of Minnesota Press, 2004, p. 42.
88 Erich Fromm, *The Fear of Freedom* (1942), London/New York: Routledge, 2005, p. 221.
89 Silverman, *Threshold of the Visible World*, p. 37.
90 Ibid., p. 31.
91 L. Hankinson Nelson, 'Epistemological communities', in L. Alcoff and E. Potter (eds.), *Feminist Epistemologies*, London/New York: Routledge, 1993, p. 121.
92 Lorraine Code, *Rhetorical Spaces: Essay on (Gendered) Locations*, New York: Routledge, 1995, p. 275.

5 The problem of entitlement

1 Sigmund Freud, 'Some character-types met with in psycho-analytic work', section I, 'The Exceptions', *Standard Edition*, 1916, vol. 14, p. 312.
2 Ibid., p. 313.
3 Joyce McDougall, personal communication at the Barcelona IPA Congress.
4 Freud, 'Some Character-Types', p. 315.
5 Ibid., p. 313.
6 Ibid., p. 314.
7 Ibid., p. 315.
8 Ibid., p. 314.
9 Simone Weil, *Gravity and Grace* (1947), trans. Emma Crawford and Mario von der Ruhr, London/New York: Routledge Classics, 2007, p. 70.
10 Donald Winnicott, *Playing and Reality*, London: Tavistock Publications, 1971, p. 68.
11 Neville Symington, *Narcissism: A New Theory*, London: Karnac, 1993, p. 108.
12 Harold Blum, '"The exceptions" reviewed: the formation and deformation of the privileged character', paper presented at the Psychoanalytic Institute of Rome (Centro Psicoanalitico di Roma) on 13 October 2000, p. 6.
13 Ibid., p. 7.
14 Ibid., p. 8.
15 Ibid., p. 9.
16 Ibid., p. 13.
17 Stuart Pizer, *Building Bridges: Negotiation of Paradox in Psychoanalysis*, Hillsdale, NJ/London: Analytic Press, 1998, p. 145.
18 Symington, *Narcissism*, p. 18.
19 Robert Nozick, *Philosophical Explanations*, Oxford: Clarendon Press, 1981, p. 4.
20 Symington, *Narcissism*, p. 53.
21 Ibid.
22 Neville Symington, *The Spirit of Sanity*, London: Karnac, 2001, p. 106.

23 Neville Symington, *A Pattern of Madness*, London: Karnac, 2002, pp. 63–4.
24 Sigmund Freud, 'The unconscious', appendix C, *Standard Edition*, 1915, vol. 14, p. 194.
25 Symington, *Narcissism*, pp. 65–6.
26 Roberta De Monticelli, *L'ordine del cuore: Etica e teoria del sentire*, Milan: Garzanti, 2003, p. 246.
27 Symington, *Narcissism*, p. 71.
28 Ibid., p. 72.
29 Joseph Epstein, *Envy: The Seven Deadly Sins*, Oxford: Oxford University Press, 2003, p. 11.
30 Martin Buber, *Good and Evil*, trans. Michael Hale Bullock, New York: Charles Scribner's Sons, 1953, p. 111.
31 Ludwig Wittgenstein, as reported in Rush Rhees, *Recollections of Wittgenstein*, Oxford: Oxford University Press, 1984. Quoted in Charles Altieri, *Subjective Agency: A Theory of First-Person Expressivity and Its Social Implications*, Oxford, UK/Cambridge, MA: Blackwell Publishers, 1994, p. 58.
32 James Grotstein, 'Foreword', in Symington, *Narcissism*, p. xvi.
33 Cf. Freud, 'Some character-types', *Standard Edition*, 1916, vol. 14, pp. 311–5.
34 Symington, *Narcissism*, p. 116.
35 Søren Kierkegaard, *The Sickness unto Death: A Christian Psychological Exposition for Upbuilding and Awakening* (1849), trans. Howard V. Hong and Edna H. Hong, Princeton, NJ: Princeton University Press, 1983, p. 19.
36 Ibid.
37 Ibid.
38 Christopher Bollas, *Cracking Up: The Work of Unconscious Experience*, London: Routledge, 1997, p. 94.
39 Ibid., p. 95.

6 Actions and reactions

1 Neville Symington deplores the reactive way of dealing with others, in *A Pattern of Madness*, London: Karnac, 2002, p. 45.
2 The probable neologism 'psychopoietic' is used to indicate vicissitudes (comparable to inner metabolic processes) that essentially sustain and contribute to the formation of our psyche.
3 W. Ury, *Getting Past NO*, New York: Bantam Books, 1991, p. 10.
4 Ibid.
5 Simone Weil, *Gravity and Grace* (1947), trans. Emma Crawford and Mario von der Ruhr, London/New York: Routledge Classics, 2007, p. 6.
6 Kelly Oliver, *The Colonization of Psychic Space: A Psychoanalytic Social Theory of Oppression*, Minneapolis, MN/London: University of Minnesota Press, 2004, p. xv.
7 Symington, *Pattern of Madness*, p. 47.
8 Weil, *Gravity and Grace*, p. 6.
9 Mary Midgley, *The Myths We Live By*, London/New York: Routledge, 2006, p. 47.
10 D. Bolton and J. Hill, *Mind, Meaning and Mental Disorder: The Nature of Causal Explanation in Psychopathology and Psychiatry*, Oxford/New York/Tokyo: Oxford University Press, 1996, pp. 13–14.
11 Symington, *Pattern of Madness*, p. 24.
12 Ibid.

13 Robert Thurman, *Anger: The Seven Deadly Sins*, New York: Public Library and Oxford University Press, 2006, p. 84.
14 Ibid., p. 85.
15 Ibid., pp. 72–3.
16 Weil, *Gravity and Grace*, p. 69.
17 Sigmund Freud, 'Preface' (to 4th edition, 1920), *Three Essays on the Theory of Sexuality, Standard Edition*, 1905, vol. 7, p. 134.
18 Thurman, *Anger*, p. 89.
19 Ibid., p. 81.
20 Julia Kristeva, *New Maladies of the Soul*, trans. Ross Guberman, New York: Columbia University Press, 1995, p. 6.
21 Weil, *Gravity and Grace*, p. 39.
22 Michael Eigen, *Toxic Nourishment*, London: Karnac, 1999, p. 49.
23 Neville Symington, *The Spirit of Sanity*, London: Karnac, 2001, p. 84.
24 Weil, *Gravity and Grace*, p. 74.

7 The question of forgiveness

1 Donald Winnicott, *Playing and Reality*, London: Tavistock, 1971, p. 69.
2 Kelly Oliver, *The Colonization of Psychic Space: A Psychoanalytic Social Theory of Oppression*, Minneapolis, MN/London: University of Minnesota Press, 2004, p. 161.
3 Ibid., p. 159.
4 Ibid., pp. 161–2.
5 Michael Howe, *Genius Explained*, Cambridge: Cambridge University Press, 1999, p. 205.
6 Oliver, *Colonization of Psychic Space*, p. 162.
7 Christopher Bollas, *Cracking Up: The Work of Unconscious Experience*, London: Routledge, 1997, pp. 4–5.
8 Ibid., p. 5.
9 Michael Eigen, 'The area of faith in Winnicott, Lacan and Bion', *International Journal of Psychoanalysis*, 1981, vol. 62, pp. 413–33.
10 Neville Symington, *Narcissism: A New Theory*, London, Karnac, 1993, p. 123.
11 Hanna Arendt, *The Human Condition*, Chicago/London: University of Chicago Press, 1998, p. 241.
12 Oliver, *Colonization of Psychic Space*, p. 180.
13 Ibid., p. xvii.
14 Winnicott, *Playing and Reality*, pp. 67–8.
15 Ibid., p. 65.
16 See Oliver, *Colonization of Psychic Space*, p. 40.
17 Michael Parsons, *The Dove that Returns, The Dove that Vanishes: Paradox and Creativity in Psychoanalysis*, The New Library of Psychoanalysis, London: Routledge, 2000, p. 24.
18 I. Berlin and H. Hardy (eds.), *Against the Current: Essays in the History of Ideas*, Oxford: Oxford University Press, 1979. Quoted in Neville Symington, *The Spirit of Sanity*, London: Karnac, 2001, p. 69.
19 Oliver, *Colonization of Psychic Space*, p. 159.
20 Winnicott, *Playing and Reality*, p. 69.
21 Oliver, *Colonization of Psychic Space*, p. 162.
22 Ibid., p. 188.
23 Ludwig Wittgenstein, *Last Writings in the Philosophy of Psychology*, vol. II, *The*

Inner and the Outer 1949–1951, trans. C. G. Luckhardt and M. Ane, ed. G. H. von Wright and H. Nyman, Oxford: Blackwell Publishers, 1992, paragraph 65e.
24 Oliver, *Colonization of Psychic Space*, p. 177.
25 Arendt, *Human Condition*, p. 238.
26 Oliver, *Colonization of Psychic Space*, p. 186.
27 Julia Kristeva, *Black Sun: Depression and Melancholy*, trans. Leon Roudiez, New York: Columbia University Press, 1989, p. 199.
28 Symington, *Narcissism*, p. 114.
29 Oliver, *Colonization of Psychic Space*, p. 181.
30 Michael Eigen, *Toxic Nourishment*, London: Karnac, 1999, p. 48.
31 Arendt, *Human Condition*, p. 240.
32 Oliver, *Colonization of Psychic Space*, p. 179.
33 Ibid., p. 92.
34 Ibid., p. 129.
35 Ibid., pp. 195–6.
36 Ibid., p. 196.
37 Arendt, *Human Condition*, p. 236.
38 Ibid., p. 237.

8 The quest for responsibility

1 A comparable thesis is developed in Maria Carmen Gear, Ernesto Caesar Liendo and Lila Lee Scott, *Dream Fulfillment*, Northvale, NJ/London: Jason Aronson, 1988, p. xi.
2 Wilfred R. Bion, *Attention and Interpretation: A Scientific Approach to Insight in Psycho-Analysis and Groups*, London: Tavistock, 1978, p. 13.
3 Neville Symington, *A Pattern of Madness*, London: Karnac, 2002, p. 40.
4 Sigmund Freud, 'Lines of advance in psycho-analytic therapy', *Standard Edition*, 1919 [1918], vol. 17, p. 161.
5 Ibid.
6 Ibid.
7 This argument is extensively developed in Gemma Corradi Fiumara, *The Mind's Affective Life: A Psychoanalytic and Philosophical Inquiry*, London/New York: Brunner-Routledge, 2001.
8 Erich Fromm, *The Fear of Freedom*, London/New York: Routledge, 2005.
9 Ibid., p. ix.
10 Ibid., p. 161.
11 Jonathan Lear, *Open Minded: Working out the Logic of the Soul*, Cambridge, MA: Harvard University Press, 1998, p. 272.
12 Sigmund Freud, *Moses and Monotheism*, essay III, 'Moses, his people and monotheist religion', part II.C, 'The advance in intellectuality', *Standard Edition*, 1938, vol. 23, p. 14, note 1.

9 Empathy and sympathy

1 See Nancy Eisenberg, *Encyclopedia of Psychology*, ed. in chief Alan E. Kazdin, Oxford, UK: Oxford University Press and American Psychological Association, 2000, vol. 3, p. 179.
2 David Black, 'Sympathy reconfigured: some reflections on sympathy, empathy and discovery of values', *International Journal of Psychoanalysis*, 2004, vol. 85, pp. 579–95.

3 See Eugenio Gaddini, 'On imitation', *International Journal of Psychoanalysis*, 1969, vol. 50, pp. 475–84.

4 *The Pocket Oxford Dictionary*, 7th edition, ed. R. E. Allen, Oxford, UK: Clarendon Press, 1985, pp. 762, 240.

5 Søren Kierkegaard, *Fear and Trembling: The Sickness unto Death*, trans. W. Lowrie, Princeton, NJ: Princeton University Press, 1974, p. 15.

6 David Hume, *A Treatise of Human Nature* (1739), ed. D. F. Norton and M. J. Norton, Oxford, UK: Oxford University Press, 2000, p. 206.

7 Ibid. In the chapter entitled 'Of will and direct passions', he also remarks: 'Few are capable of distinguishing betwixt the liberty of *spontaneity* . . . and the liberty of *indifference*; betwixt that which is oppos'd to violence, and that which means a negation of necessity and causes.' *A Treatise of Human Nature: Being an Attempt to Introduce the Experimental Method of Reasoning into Moral Subjects* (1739), ed. L. A. Selby-Bigge, Oxford, UK: Clarendon Press, 1967, part III, p. 407.

8 Sigmund Freud, *Group Psychology and the Analysis of the Ego, Standard Edition*, 1917, vol. 14, p. 108.

9 Black, 'Sympathy Reconfigured'.

10 This issue is extensively discussed in Gemma Corradi Fiumara, *The Metaphoric Process: Connections between Language and Life*, London/New York: Routledge, 1995, chapter 4, 'The oppositional metaphor', comprising sections 1 'On being right in arguments', 2 'Agreement and disagreement', and 3 'Controversial zeal', pp. 42–51.

11 Edith Stein, *On the Problem of Empathy*, trans. Waltrout Stein, 2nd edition, The Hague: Martinus Nijhoff, 1970, p. 7.

12 Ibid.

13 Ibid., p. 23.

14 Ibid., p. 17. She also remarks (p. 18): 'I would like to call attention to just one more concept from Lipp's description: that which he designates as "reflective sympathy" and which I would like to call the reiteration of empathy, more exactly, a particular case of reiteration. . . . And so I can also empathize with the empathized, i.e., among the acts of another that I grasp empathically there can be empathic acts in which the other grasps another's acts. This "other" can be a third person or me myself.'

15 See Neville Symington, *Narcissism: A New Theory*, London: Karnac, 1993, p. 39. This central issue is discussed throughout his book.

16 Black, 'Sympathy reconfigured'.

17 Symington, *Narcissism*, p. 101.

18 See Kaja Silverman, *The Threshold of the Visible World*, London/New York: Routledge, 1996, p. 39.

19 See Neville Symington, *The Spirit of Sanity*, London, Karnac, 2001, p. 43. The question is whether this refusal of otherness is permanent and fatal or else whether it can be revisited and renegotiated. But then, what is analysis if not the ever-renewed attempt to restructure our basic attitudes? Analysts are not there to give advice or to pursue their specific goals but, rather, to sustain the development of a more realistic relationship to the 'reality' of others and to the 'reality' of one's profound self. This is, of course, a never-ending enterprise; the route in the proper direction, however, has to be constantly corrected and re-adjusted in the vicissitudes of life. This complexive attitude is conducive to empathic actions rather than sympathetic reactions.

20 See Ignacio Matte Blanco, *The Unconscious as Infinite Sets: An Essay in Bi-Logic*, London: Duckworth, 1975.

21 Jessica Benjamin, *Shadow of the Other: Intersubjectivity and Gender in Psychoanalysis*, London/New York: Routledge, 1998, p. xviii.

22 See Robert Caper, 'A mind of one's own', *International Journal of Psychoanalysis*, vol. 72(2), 1997, pp. 265–78.

23 See Stefano Bolognini, 'Empathy and "empathism"', *International Journal of Psychoanalysis*, vol. 78, 1997, pp. 279–93.

24 Michael Eigen, 'The area of faith in Winnicott, Lacan and Bion', *International Journal of Psychoanalysis*, vol. 62, 1981, pp. 413–33.

25 See Corradi Fiumara, *Metaphoric Process*, chapter 10, 'Vicissitudes of Self Formation', and especially section 3, 'Primal interaction', pp. 125–42.

26 Wilfred R. Bion, *Attention and Interpretation: A Scientific Approach to Insight in Psycho-Analysis*, London: Tavistock Publications, 1978, p. 105.

27 Max Scheler, *The Nature of Sympathy*, trans. Peter Heath, Hamden, CT: Archon Press, 1970, pp. 21–2.

28 Burness E. Moore and Bernard D. Fine (eds.), *Psychoanalytic Terms and Concepts*, New Haven, CT/London: The American Psychoanalytic Association and Yale University Press, 1990, p. 67.

29 Sigmund Freud, 'Dostoevsky and parricide', *Standard Edition*, 1927, vol. 21, pp. 189–90. Freud also remarks: 'The comic effect depends . . . on the *difference* between the two cathectic expenditures – one's own and the other person's as estimated by "empathy" – and not on which of the two the difference favours.' *Jokes and Their Relation to the Unconscious*', *Standard Edition*, 1905, vol. 7, p. 195. Further on he says: 'But it is noteworthy that we only find someone's being put in a position of inferiority comic where there is empathy' (ibid., p. 197).

30 On this topic see Gemma Corradi Fiumara, *The Mind's Affective Life: A Psychoanalytic and Philosophical Inquiry*, London/New York: Routledge, 2001, especially chapter 2, 'From Philosophy to Epistemophily', pp. 20–32.

31 Neville Symington, *A Pattern of Madness*, London: Karnac, 2002, p. 21.

32 Benjamin, *Shadow of the Other*, p. xiii.

33 Ibid., p. 85.

34 Ibid., p. 6.

35 This issue is discussed in Symington, *Spirit of Sanity*, p. 74.

36 Eigen, 'The area of faith in Winnicott, Lacan and Bion'.

37 Simone Weil, *Gravity and Grace*, trans. Emma Crawford and Mario von der Ruhr, London/New York: Routledge Classics, 2007, p. 65.

38 This is the central thesis in Christopher Bollas, *The Shadow of the Object: Psychoanalysis of the Unthought Known*, London: Free Association Books, 1987.

39 Lorraine Code, 'Introduction: why feminists do not read Gadamer', in Lorraine Code (ed.), *Feminist Interpretations of Hans-Georg Gadamer*, University Park, PA: Pennsylvania State University Press, 2003, pp. 1–36.

40 This is one of the main issues in Jeremy Rifkin, *The European Dream: How Europe's Vision of the Future Is Quickly Eclipsing the American Dream*, Cambridge, UK: Polity Press, 2004. See, for instance, p. 271.

41 Evelyne Fox Keller, *Reflections on Gender and Science*, New Haven, CT: Yale University Press, 1985, p. 194.

42 Susan Bordo, 'The Cartesian masculinization of thought', in Sandra Harding and Jean F. O'Ban (eds.), *Sex and Scientific Inquiry*, Chicago: University of Chicago Press, 1987, p. 11.

43 Silverman, *Threshold of the Visible World*, p. 26.

44 On this question, see Howard Gardner, *Five Minds for the Future*, Boston, MA: Harvard Business School Press, 2006 [Italian trans., Ester Dornetti, *Cinque chiavi per il futuro*, Milan: Feltrinelli, 2007].

45 On the critical importance of listening, see Gemma Corradi Fiumara, *The Other Side of Language: A Philosophy of Listening*, London/New York: Routledge, 1990.
46 Galileo Galilei, *Dialogue on the Great World Systems*, trans. George de Santillana, Chicago: University of Chicago Press, 1953, pp. 116–7.
47 L. Hankinson Nelson, 'Epistemological communities', in L. Alcoff and E. Potter (eds.), *Feminist Epistemologies*, London/New York: Routledge, 1993, p. 122.
48 Ibid.
49 Ibid., pp. 121–2.
50 Aristotle, *Poetics*, paragraph 22, 1457b, 6–9, *The Complete Works of Aristotle*, Revised Oxford Translation ed. J. Barnes, vol. II, Bollingen Series LXXX 1.2, Princeton, NJ: Princeton University Press, 1985, p. 2234.
51 Ibid., paragraph 22, 1459a, 5–8, p. 2235.
52 Aristotle, *Rhetoric*, ibid., 10–15, p. 2239.
53 This thesis has been presented in Corradi Fiumara, *Metaphoric Process*, p. 2.
54 See Gardner, *Five Minds* [*Cinque chiavi per il futuro*, p. 57].
55 Ibid.
56 Mary Midgley, *The Myths We Live By*, London/New York: Routledge, 2006, p. 22.

10 Self-formation and self-decreation

1 This argument is developed in Michael Parsons, *The Dove that Returns, the Dove that Vanishes: Paradox and Creativity in Psychoanalysis*, London: Routledge, 2000, p. 4.
2 See Gemma Corradi Fiumara, *The Other Side of Language: A Philosophy of Listening*, chapter 4, section 4, 'A differentiation between the concepts of power and strength', and section 5, 'On the accepted meaning of "strong" and "weak" in western culture', London/New York: Routledge, 1990, pp. 62–71.
3 Parsons, *The Dove that Returns*, p. 43.
4 Ibid.
5 This issue is discussed in Gemma Corradi Fiumara, *The Metaphoric Process: Connections between Language and Life*, chapter 10, 'Vicissitudes of Self-Formation', London/New York: Routledge, 1995, pp. 125–42.
6 See Melanie Klein, 'The Oedipus Complex in the light of early anxieties', in *Contributions to Psycho-Analysis 1921–1945*, London: Hogarth Press and The Institute of Psycho-Analysis, 1973, pp. 339–90.
7 A comparable discussion is presented in Gemma Corradi Fiumara, chapter 10, section 1, 'The experiences of loss', in *The Symbolic Function: Psychoanalysis and the Philosophy of Language*, Oxford, UK/Cambridge, MA: Blackwell Publishers, 1992, pp. 134–43.
8 Corradi Fiumara, *Metaphoric Process*, p. 123.
9 This is the title of the book by G. Lakoff and M. Johnson, *Metaphors We Live By*, Chicago/London: University of Chicago Press, 1980.
10 Francis Bacon, *Novum Organon*, XLVI, quoted in Stephen Denning, *The Secret Language of Leadership*, San Francisco, CA: Jossey-Bass, 2007.
11 Carl Gustav Jung, 'The Soul and Death', in *The Collected Works of C.G. Jung*, vol. 8, *The Structure and Dynamics of the Psyche*, trans. R. F. C. Hull, ed. H. Read, M. Fordham and G. Adler, London: Routledge & Kegan Paul, 1960, p. 407.

12 See Corradi Fiumara, *Symbolic Function*, p. 78.
13 This point is made by Jonathan Lear, *Open Minded: Working Out the Logic of the Soul*, Cambridge, MA: Harvard University Press, 1990, p. 81.
14 Michael Eigen, *Toxic Nourishment*, London: Karnac, 1999, pp. 15–16.

Bibliography

Alighieri, D. (1958) *The Inferno of Dante Alighieri*, The Temple Classics, London/ New York: J. M. Dent and Sons, Aldine House.

Altieri, C. (1994) *Subjective Agency: A Theory of First-Person Expressivity and Its Social Implications*, Oxford, UK/Cambridge, MA: Blackwell Publishers.

Andersson, K. E. and Sahlin, N. E. (eds.) (1997) *The Complexity of Creativity*, London: Routledge.

Arendt, H. (1978) *The Life of the Mind*, vol. 1, *Thinking*, San Diego, CA: Harcourt-Brace-Jovanovich.

Arendt, H. (1978) *The Life of the Mind*, vol. 2, *Willing*, San Diego, CA: Harcourt-Brace-Jovanovich.

Arendt, H. (1998) *The Human Condition*, with an introduction by Margaret Canovan, Chicago/London: University of Chicago Press.

Aristotle (1957) *De interpretatione*, ed. E. Riondato, Padova: Editrice Antenore.

Aristotle (1985) *Poetics: The Complete Works of Aristotle*, vol. 2, revised Oxford translation, ed. J. Barnes, Bollingen Series LXXXI.2, Princeton, NJ: Princeton University Press.

Aulagnier, P. (2001) *The Violence of Interpretation: From Pictogram to Statement*, trans. A. Sheridan, London/New York: Brunner-Routledge, in association with the Institute of Psychoanalysis.

Bacon, F. (1974) *The Advancement of Learning and New Atlantis*, A. Johnston (ed.), Oxford: Clarendon Press.

Benjamin, J. (1990) *The Bonds of Love: Psychoanalysis, Feminism and the Problem of Domination*, London: Virago.

Benjamin, J. (1998) *Shadow of the Other: Intersubjectivity and Gender in Psycho-Analysis*, London: Routledge.

Berlin, I. and Hardy, H. (eds.) (1979) *Against the Current: Essays in the History of Ideas*, Oxford: Oxford University Press.

Bernardi, R. (1995) 'The role of paradigmatic determinants in psychoanalytic understanding', *International Journal of Psychoanalysis*, 70: 341–57.

Bion, W. R. (1962) 'A theory of thinking', *International Journal of Psychoanalysis*, 43: 306–10.

Bion, W. R. (1967) *Second Thoughts*, New York: Jason Aronson.

Bion, W. R. (1978) *Attention and Interpretation: A Scientific Approach to Insight in Psycho-Analysis and Groups*, London: Tavistock.

Black, D. (2004) 'Sympathy reconfigured: Some reflections on sympathy, empathy and the discovery of values', *International Journal of Psychoanalysis*, 85: 579–95.

Blum, H. P. (2000) 'The exceptions reviewed: The formation and deformation of the privileged character', paper presented at the Psychoanalytic Institute of Rome.

Bollas, C. (1987) *The Shadow of the Object: Psychoanalysis of the Unthought Known*, London: Free Association Books.

Bollas, C. (1991) *The Forces of Destiny: Psychoanalysis and Human Idiom*, London: Free Association Press.

Bollas, C. (1993) *Being a Character: Psychoanalysis and Self Experience*, London: Routledge.

Bollas, C. (1997) *Cracking Up: The Work of Unconscious Experience*, London: Routledge.

Bollas, C. (1999) *The Mystery of Things*, London: Brunner-Routledge.

Bolognini, S. (1997) 'Empathy and empathism', *International Journal of Psycho-Analysis*, 78: 279–93.

Bolton, D. and Hill, J. (1996) *Mind, Meaning and Mental Disorder: The Nature of Causal Explanation in Psychology and Psychiatry*, Oxford/New York/Tokyo: Oxford University Press.

Bordo, S. (1987) 'The Cartesian masculinization of thought', in S. Harding and J. F. O'Barr (eds.), *Sex and Scientific Inquiry*, Chicago: University of Chicago Press.

Bregman, L. (1986) 'Death and its denial: Definitions and perspectives from depth psychology and Christian thought', *Thought*, 61: 150–61.

Britton, R. (1998) *Belief and Imagination: Explorations in Psychoanalysis*, London/New York: Routledge, in association with the Institute of Psychoanalysis.

Buber, M. (1953) *Good and Evil*, trans. M. H. Bullock, New York: Charles Scribner's Sons.

Campbell, R. and Sowden, L. (eds.) (1985) *Paradoxes of Rationality and Cooperation: Prisoner's Dilemma and Newcomb's Problem*, Vancouver: University of British Columbia Press.

Caper, R. (1997) 'A mind of one's own', *International Journal of Psychoanalysis*, 72, 2: 265–78.

Caper, R. (1999) *A Mind of One's Own: A Kleinian View of Self and Object*, The New Library of Psychoanalysis, London/New York: Routledge.

Casement, P. (2002) *Learning from Our Mistakes: Beyond Dogma in Psychoanalysis and Psychotherapy*, London: Brunner-Routledge.

Cassam, Q. (ed.) (2004) *Self Knowledge*, Oxford: Oxford University Press.

Cavell, M. (2006) *Becoming a Subject: Reflections in Philosophy and Psychoanalysis*, Oxford: Oxford University Press.

Chamberlain, L. (2000) *The Secret Artist: A Close Reading of Sigmund Freud*, London: Quartet Books.

Civin, M. (2000) *Male, Female, Email: The Struggle for Relatedness in a Paranoid Society*, New York: Other Press.

Code, L. (1995) *Rhetorical Spaces: Essay on (Gendered) Locations*, New York: Routledge.

Code, L. (ed.) (2003) 'Introduction: Why feminists do not read Gadamer', in *Feminist Interpretations of Hans-Georg Gadamer*, University Park, PA: Pennsylvania State University Press.

Cohen, J. (2001) *Apart from Freud: Notes for a Rational Psychoanalysis*, San Francisco, CA: City Lights Books.

Corradi Fiumara, G. (1990) *The Other Side of Language: A Philosophy of Listening*, London/New York: Routledge.

Corradi Fiumara, G. (1992) *The Symbolic Function: Psychoanalysis and the Philosophy of Language*, Oxford, UK/Cambridge, MA: Blackwell Publishers.

Corradi Fiumara, G. (1995) *The Metaphoric Process: Connections between Language and Life*, London/New York: Routledge.

Corradi Fiumara, G. (2001) *The Mind's Affective Life: A Psychoanalytic and Philosophical Inquiry*, London/New York: Brunner-Routledge.

Davies, J. M. and Frawley, M. G. (1994) *Treating the Adult Survivor of Childhood Sexual Abuse: A Psychoanalytic Perspective*, New York: Basic Books.

De Monticelli, R. (2003) *L'ordine del cuore: Etica e teoria del sentire*, Milan: Garzanti.

Denning, S. (2007) *The Secret Language of Leadership*, San Francisco, CA: Jossey-Bass.

Edelman, G. M. (1987) *Neural Darwinism*, New York: Basic Books.

Edelman, G. M. (1989) *The Remembered Present*, New York: Basic Books.

Egidi, M. R. (2005) 'G.H. von Wright on self determination and free agency', in E. Niiniluoto and R. Vilkko (eds.) *Philosophical Essays in Memoriam George Henrik von Wright*, Acta Philosophica Fennica, 77, Helsinki: 105–14.

Eigen, M. (1981) 'The area of faith in Winnicott, Lacan and Bion', *International Journal of Psychoanalysis*, 62: 413–33.

Eigen, M. (1996) *Psychic Deadness*, Northvale, NJ/London: Jason Aronson.

Eigen, M. (1999) *Toxic Nourishment*, London: Karnac.

Eigen, M. (2004) *Damaged Bonds*, London/New York: Karnac.

Eisenberg, N. (2000) *Encyclopaedia of Psychology*, ed. A. E. Kazdin, Oxford: Oxford University Press and American Psychological Association.

Eisenberg, N. and Stranger, J. (eds.) (1987) *Empathy and Its Development*, Cambridge, UK: Cambridge University Press.

Ekman, P. (2003) *Gripped by Emotion*, New York: Times Books and Henry Holt.

Emmons, R. A. (1999) *The Psychology of Ultimate Concerns: Motivation and Spirituality in Personality*, London: Guilford Press.

Epstein, J. (2003) *Envy: The Seven Deadly Sins*, Oxford, UK: Oxford University Press.

Faimberg, H. (2008) *Ascoltando tre generazioni: Legami narcisistici e identificazioni alienanti*, Milan: Franco Angeli.

Feinman, R. P. (2001) *The Pleasure of Finding Things Out*, New York: Penguin Books.

Ferenczi, S. (1952) 'Introjection and transference', in *First Contributions to Psycho-Analysis*, London: Hogarth Press.

Flanagan, O. (2002) *The Problem of the Soul: Two Visions of Mind and How to Reconcile Them*, New York: Basic Books.

Fonagy, P., Gergely, G., Jurist, E. L. and Target, M. (2002) *Affect Regulation, Mentalization, and the Development of the Self*, New York: Other Press.

Fox-Keller, E. (1985) *Reflections on Gender and Science*, New Haven, CT: Yale University Press.

Fromm, E. (2005) *The Fear of Freedom*, London/New York: Routledge.

Freud, S. All references are to *The Standard Edition of the Complete Psychological Works of Sigmund Freud*, vols. 1–24, trans. and ed. J. Strachey in collaboration with A. Freud, London: Hogarth Press and the Institute of Psycho-Analysis, 1953–1974.

Freud, S. (1889) 'Review of August Forel's *Hypnotism*', *Standard Edition*, vol. 1.

Freud, S. (1901) *Psychopathology of Everyday Life*, chapter 12, 'Determinism, belief in chance and superstition – [on] some points of view', *Standard Edition*, vol. 6.

Freud, S. (1905) *Jokes and Their Relation to the Unconscious*, *Standard Edition*, vol. 7.

Freud, S. (1911) 'Formulation on the two principles of mental functioning', *Standard Edition*, vol. 12.

Freud, S. (1915) 'The unconscious', appendix C, 'Words and things', *Standard Edition*, vol. 14.

Freud, S. (1915) *Introductory Lectures on Psycho-Analysis*, lecture II, 'Parapraxes', *Standard Edition*, vol. 15.

Freud, S. (1916) 'Some character-types met with in psychoanalytic work', section I, 'The exceptions', *Standard Edition*, vol. 14.

Freud, S. (1917 [1915]) 'Mourning and melancholia', *Standard Edition*, vol. 14.

Freud, S. (1919 [1918]) 'Lines of advance in psycho-analytic therapy', *Standard Edition*, vol. 17.

Freud, S. (1921) *Group Psychology and the Analysis of the Ego*, part II, 'Le Bon's description of the group mind', *Standard Edition*, vol. 18.

Freud, S. (1921) *Group Psychology and the Analysis of the Ego*, part VIII, 'Identification', *Standard Edition*, vol. 18.

Freud, S. (1927) 'Dostoevsky and parricide', *Standard Edition*, vol. 21.

Freud, S. (1930) 'The Goethe Prize. Address delivered in the Goethe House at Frankfurt, 1930', *Standard Edition*, vol. 21.

Freud, S. (1939) *Moses and Monotheism*, essay III, 'Moses, his people and monotheist religion. Part II.C, The advance in intellectuality', *Standard Edition*, vol. 23.

Gaddini, E. (1969) 'On imitation', *International of Journal of Psycho-Analysis*, 50: 475–84.

Galileo Galilei (1953) *Dialogue on the Great World Systems*, the Salisbury translation, revised, annotated and with an introduction by G. de Santillana, Chicago: University of Chicago Press.

Gamble, S. (ed.) (2001) *The Routledge Companion to Feminism and Postfeminism*, London: Routledge.

Gardner, H. (2007) *Cinque chiavi per il futuro*, trans. E. Dornetti, Milan: Feltrinelli.

Gear, M. C., Liendo, E. C. and Lee Scott, L. (1988) *Dream Fulfilment*, Northvale, NJ/London: Jason Aronson.

Goldie, P. (2000) *The Emotions: A Philosophical Exploration*, Oxford: Clarendon Press.

Goleman, D. (2006) *Social Intelligence: The New Science of Human Relationships*, London: Hutchison and the Random House Group.

Greenberg, L. S. and Pavio, S. C. (2004) *Working with Emotions in Psychotherapy*, London: Brunner-Routledge.

Grotstein, J. S. (1993) 'Foreword', in N. Symington, *Narcissim: A New Theory*, London: Karnac.

Hankinson, N. L. (1993) 'Epistemological communities', in L. Alcoff and E. Potter (eds.) *Feminist Epistemologies*, London/New York: Routledge.

Hanly, C. (1999) 'Subjectivity and objectivity in psychoanalysis', *Journal of the American Psychoanalytic Association*, 47: 427–45.

Hargreaves, E. and Varchevker, A. (2004) *In Pursuit of Psychic Change*, The Betty Joseph Workshop, London: Brunner-Routledge.

Hartsock, N. (1987) 'Rethinking modernism and minority versus majority theories', *Cultural Critique*, 7: 187–202.

Hayes, S. C. (2004) *Acceptance and Commitment: An Experiential Approach to Behaviour Change*, London: Brunner-Routledge.

Hesse, H. (1997) *La nevrosi si può vincere*, trans. O. Bernardi, Milan: Mondadori.

Hillman, J. (1972) *The Myth of Analysis*, Urbana, IL: North Western University Press.

Hoffman, M. (1982) 'Development of prosocial motivation: Empathy and guilt', in N. Eisenberg (ed.) *The Development of Prosocial Behaviour*, New York: Academic Press.

Hoffman, I. Z. (1998) *Ritual and Spontaneity in the Psychoanalytic Process*, Hillsdale, NJ/London: Analytic Press.

Howe, M. (1999) *Genius Explained*, Cambridge, UK: Cambridge University Press.

Hume, D. (1739/1967) *A Treatise of Human Nature: Being an Attempt to Introduce the Experimental Method of Reasoning into Moral Subjects*, ed. L. A. Selby-Bigge, Oxford, UK: Clarendon Press.

Hume, D. (1739/2000) *A Treatise of Human Nature*, ed. D. F. Norton and M. J. Norton, Oxford, UK: Oxford University Press.

Jung, C. G. (1960) 'The soul and death', in *The Collected Works of C.G. Jung*, vol. 8, *The Structure and Dynamics of the Psyche*, trans. R. F. C. Hull, ed. H. Read, M. Fordham and G. Adler, London: Routledge & Kegan Paul.

Jung, C. G. (1977) 'The Tavistock Lectures: Lecture III', in *The Collected Works of C.G. Jung*, vol. 18, *The Symbolic Life*, trans. R. F. C. Hull, ed. H. Read, M. Fordham and G. Adler, London: Routledge & Kegan Paul.

Kelman, H. (1987) 'On resonant cognition', *International Review of Psychoanalysis*, 14: 111–23.

Kierkegaard, S. (1983) *The Sickness unto Death: A Christian Psychological Exposition for Upbuilding and Awakening*, ed. and trans. H. V. Hong and E. H. Hong, Princeton, NJ: Princeton University Press.

Kitron, D. (2001) 'Secluded lives: The shelter of false selves in sociocultural contexts', *Psychoanalysis and Contemporary Thought*, 24: 67–80.

Klauber, J. (1981) *Difficulties in the Analytic Encounter*, New York: Jason Aronson.

Klein, M. (1928) 'Early stages in the Oedipus conflict', in *Contributions to Psycho-Analysis 1921–1945*, with an introduction by E. Jones, London: Hogarth Press and the Institute of Psycho-Analysis, 1973.

Klein, M. (1933) 'The early development of conscience in the child', in *Contributions to Psycho-Analysis 1921–1945*, with an introduction by E. Jones, London: Hogarth Press and the Institute of Psycho-Analysis, 1973.

Klein, M. (1957) *Envy and Gratitude*, London: Tavistock Publications.

Kolodny, S. (2000) *The Captive Muse: On Creativity and Its Inhibitions*, Madison, CT: Psychosocial Press.

Kris, A. (1976) 'On wanting too much: The "exceptions" revisited', *International Journal of Psychoanalysis*, 57: 85–95.

Kristeva, J. (1995) *New Maladies of the Soul*, trans. R. Guberman, New York: Columbia University Press.

Kristeva, J. (2000) *The Sense and Non-Sense of Revolt*, trans. J. Herman, New York: Columbia University Press.

Kumin, J. M. (1978) 'Developmental aspects of opposites and paradox', *International Review of Psychoanalysis*, 5: 477–84.

La Forgia, M. and Marozza, M. I. (2000) *L'altro e la sua mente*, Rome: Fioriti Editore.

Laplanche, J. (1976) *Life and Death in Psychoanalysis*, Baltimore, MD/London: Johns Hopkins University Press.

Lear, J. (1998) *Open Minded: Working Out the Logic of the Soul*, Cambridge, MA: Harvard University Press.

Lear, J. (1998) *Love and Its Place in Nature: A Philosophical Interpretation of Freudian Psychoanalysis*, New Haven, CT/London: Yale University Press.

Le Doux, J. E. (1996) *The Emotional Brain*, New York: Simon & Schuster.

Le Doux, J. E. (2002) *Synaptic Self: How Our Brains Become Who We Are*, New York: Viking and Penguin.

Loewenthal, D. and Snell, R. (2004) *Post-Modernism for Psychotherapists: A Critical Reader*, London: Brunner-Routledge.

Malaguti, E. (2008) *Educarsi alla resilienza: Come affrontare crisi, difficoltà e migliorarsi*, Trent, Italy: Edizioni Erickson.

Malcolm, J. (1981) *Psychoanalysis: The Impossible Profession*, New York: Alfred A. Knopf.

Marchesini, R. (2002) *Post-human: Verso nuovi modelli di esistenza*, Turin: Boringhieri.

Martin, D. (1973) *Two Critiques of Spontaneity*, Welwyn Garden City, UK: Broadwater Press.

Matte Blanco, I. (1975) *The Unconscious as Infinite Sets: An Essay in Bi-Logic*, London: Duckworth.

Matte Blanco, I. (1989) *Thinking, Feeling and Being: Clinical Reflections on the Fundamental Antinomy of Human Beings and World*, The New Library of Psychoanalysis, London: Routledge.

Mattioli, G. (2000) *La nuova frontiera della psicoanalisi: L'emozione si fa scienza*, Rome: Borla.

McDougall, J. (1986) *Theatres of the Mind: Illusion and Truth on the Psychoanalytic Stage*, London: Free Association Books.

McDougall, J. (1995) *The Many Faces of Eros: A Psychoanalytic Exploration of Human Sexuality*, London: Free Association Books.

McDowell, J. (1994) *Mind and World*, Cambridge, MA: Harvard University Press.

Mearcs, R. (2000) *Intimacy and Alienation: Memory, Trauma and Personal Being*, London: Routledge.

Meltzer, D. (1986) *Studies in Extended Metapsychology*, Strath Tay, UK: Clunie Press.

Memmi, A. (1967) *The Colonizer and the Colonized*, Boston, MA: Beacon Press.

Midgley, M. (2006) *The Myths: We Live By*, London/New York: Routledge.

Milner, M. (as Joanna Field) (1934) *A Life of One's Own*, London: Virago.

Mitchell, S. (1995) *Hope and Dread in Psychoanalysis*, New York: Basic Books.

Mitchell, S. and Aron, L. (2002) *Psicoanalisi relazionale*, vol. 1, *L'intersoggettività nell'esperienza clinica*, Turin: Boringhieri.

Mitrani, J. L. (2001) *Ordinary People and Extra-Ordinary Protections: A Post-Kleinian Approach to the Treatment of Primitive Mental States*, The New Library of Psychoanalysis, London: Brunner-Routledge.

Modell, A. (1991) 'The therapeutic relation as a paradoxical experience', *Psychoanalytic Dialogue*, 1: 13–28.

Modell, A. (1996) *The Private Self*, Cambridge, MA/London: Harvard University Press.

Money-Kyrle, R. (2002) *Scritti 1927–1977*, Turin: Boringhieri.

Moore, B. E. and Fine, B. D. (eds.) (1990) *Psychoanalytic Terms and Concepts*, New Haven, CT/London: The American Psychoanalytic Association and Yale University Press.

Moran, F. (1993) *Subject and Agency in Psychoanalysis; Which Is to Be Master?*, New York: New York University Press.

More, E. and Milligan, M. (eds.) (1994) *The Empathic Practitioner: Empathy, Gender, and Medicine*, New Brunswick, NJ: Rutgers University Press.

Nandy, A. (1983) *The Intimate Enemy: The Loss and Recovery of Self under Colonialism*, Oxford, UK: Oxford University Press.

Napier, A. D. (1986) *Masks, Transformation, and Paradox*, Berkeley, CA: University of California Press.

Nietzsche, F. (1967) *On the Genealogy of Morals*, trans. W. Kaufmann, New York: Random House.

Nozick, R. (1981) *Philosophical Explanations*, Oxford, UK: Clarendon Press.

Oksenberg Rorty, A. (2001) *The Many Faces of Evil: Historical Perspectives*, London/New York: Routledge.

Oliver, K. (2004) *The Colonization of Psychic Space: A Psychoanalytic Social Theory of Oppression*, Minneapolis, MN/London: University of Minnesota Press.

Parsons, M. (1999) 'The logic of play in psychoanalysis', *International Journal of Psychoanalysis*, 80: 871–84.

Parsons, M. (2000) *The Dove that Returns, The Dove that Vanishes: Paradox and Creativity in Psychoanalysis*, The New Library of Psychoanalysis, London: Routledge.

Pizer, S. A. (1998) *Building Bridges: The Negotiation of Paradox in Psychoanalysis*, Hillsdale, NJ/London: Analytic Press.

Premack, D. and Premack, A. (2003) *Original Intelligence: Unlocking the Mystery of Who We Are*, New York: McGraw-Hill.

Putnam, H. (1999) *The Threefold Cord: Mind, Body and World*, New York: Columbia University Press.

Quinodoz, D. (1997) *Emotional Vertigo: Between Anxiety and Pleasure*, trans. A. Pomerans, The New Library of Psychoanalysis, London/New York: Routledge.

Rayner, E. (1981) 'Infinite experiences, affects and the characteristics of the unconscious', *International Journal of Psychoanalysis*, 65: 403–12.

Rescher, N. (2001) *Paradoxes: Their Roots, Range and Resolution*, Chicago/La Salle, IL: Open Court and Corns Publishing Company.

Ricoeur, P. (1993) *Sé come un altro*, trans. D. Jannotta, Milan: Jaca Book.

Ricoeur, P. (2003) *La memoria, la storia, l'oblio*, trans. D. Jannotta, Milan: Raffaello Cortina Editore.

Rifkin, J. (2004) *The European Dream: How Europe's Vision of the Future is Quickly Eclipsing the American Dream*, Cambridge, UK: Polity Press.

Rizzuto, A. M., Meissner, W. W. and Buie, D. H. (2004) *The Dynamics of Human Aggression: Theoretical Foundations, Clinical Implications*, New York/Hove: Brunner-Routledge.

Rose, J. (2004) *On Not Being Able to Sleep: Psychoanalysis and the Modern World*, London: Vintage.

Rosenthal, D. M. (ed.) (1991) *The Nature of Mind*, New York/Oxford, UK: Oxford University Press.

Rothstein, A. (1977) 'The ego attitude of entitlement', *International Review of Psychoanalysis*, 4: 409–17.

Ryle, G. (1961) *Dilemmas*, Cambridge, UK: Cambridge University Press.

Salimbene de Adam of Parma (1946) 'Chronicon Parmense. Avvenimenti tra il 1167 e il 1287', in A.Viscardi *et al.* (eds.) *La Letteratura italiana: Storia e testi. Le origini*, Milan/Naples: Ricciardi Editore.

Sandler, J. and Dreher, A. U. (1996) *What Do Psychoanalysts Want: The Problem of Aim in Psychoanalytic Therapy*, London/New York: Routledge, in association with the Institute of Psycho-Analysis.

Schaefer, R. (1978) *A New Language for Psychoanalysis*, New Haven, CT: Yale University Press.

Scheler, M. (1970) *The Nature of Sympathy*, trans. P. Heath, Hamden, CT: Archon Press.

Scheler, M. (1999) *Il valore della vita emotiva*, Milan: Guerini.

Scheman, N. (1993) *Engenderings: Constructions of Knowledge, Authority and Privilege*, London/New York: Routledge.

Schilpp, P. A. and Hahn, L. E. (eds.) (1989) *The Philosophy of Georg Henrik von Wright*, La Salle, IL: Open Court Press.

Schleiermacher, F. D. E. (1968) *Ermeneutica*, trans. M. Marassi, Milan: Rusconi.

Silverman, K. (1996) *The Threshold of the Visible World*, London/New York: Routledge.

Spence, D. (1987) 'Turning happenings into meanings: The central role of the self', in P. Young-Eisendrath and J. Hall (eds.), *The Book of the Self: Person, Pretext and Process*, New York: New York University Press.

Spence, D. (1999) *La voce retorica della psicoanalisi*, Rome: Fioriti Editore.

Stein, E. (1970) *On the Problem of Empathy*, trans. W. Stein, with a foreword by E. W. Straus; second edition, The Hague: Martinus Nijhoff.

Stern, D. N., Sander, L. W., Nahum, J. P., Harrison, A. M., Lyons-Ruth, K., Morgan, A. C. *et al.* (1998) 'Non-interpretative mechanisms in psychoanalytic therapy: The "something more" than interpretation', *International Journal of Psychoanalysis*, 79: 903–21.

Strachey, J. (1934) 'The nature of the therapeutic action of psycho-analysis', *International Journal of Psychoanalysis*, 15: 127–59.

Summers, F. (1994) *Object Relations: Theories and Psychopathology. A Comprehensive Text*, Hillsdale, NJ: Analytic Press.

Symington, N. (1993) *Narcissism: A New Theory*, London: Karnac.

Symington, N. (2001) *The Spirit of Sanity*, London: Karnac.

Symington, N. (2002) *A Pattern of Madness*, London: Karnac.

Thurman, R. A. F. (2006) *Anger: The Seven Deadly Sins*, New York: New York Public Library and Oxford University Press.

Toulmin, S. (2001) *Return to Reason*, Cambridge, MA: Harvard University Press.

Tustin, F. (1972) *Autism and Childhood Psychosis*, London: Hogarth Press.

Ury, W. (1991) *Getting Past No*, New York: Bantam Books.

Vigotsky, L. (1997) *Thought and Language*, ed. and revised by A. Kozulin, Cambridge, MA: MIT Press.

von Wright, G. H. (1971) *Explanation and Understanding*, London: Routledge & Kegan Paul.

von Wright, G. H. (1998) *Of Human Freedom in the Shadow of Descartes*, Dordrecht: Kluwer.

Weil, S. (1947) *Gravity and Grace*, trans. E. Crawford and M. von der Ruhr, with an introduction and postscript by G. Thibon, London/New York: Routledge Classics.

Williams, B. (1973) *Problems of the Self: Philosophical Papers 1956–1972*, Cambridge, UK: Cambridge University Press.

Winnicott, D. W. (1965) *The Maturational Processes and the Facilitating Environment*, New York: International Universities Press.

Winnicott, D. W. (1971) *Playing and Reality*, London: Tavistock Publications.

Winnicott, D. W. (1989) *Psychoanalytic Explorations*, ed. C. Winnicott, R. Shepherd and M. Davis, Cambridge, MA: Harvard University Press.

Wittgenstein, L. (1992) *Last Writings on the Philosophy of Psychology*, vol. 2, *The Inner and the Outer 1949–1951*, trans. C. G. Luckhardt and M. A. E. Ane, ed. G. H. von Wright and H. Nyman, Oxford, UK: Blackwell Publishers.

Wright, E. (2006) *Psychoanalytic Criticism: A Reappraisal*, Cambridge, UK: Polity Press.

Index